WHY LIBERALISM FAILED

Why Liberalism Failed

PATRICK J. DENEEN

Foreword by James Davison Hunter and
John M. Owen IV

Yale
UNIVERSITY PRESS
New Haven and London

Published with the assistance of the Institute for Advanced Studies in Culture, University of Virginia.

Yale University Press books may be purchased in quantity for educational, business, or promotional use. For information, please e-mail sales.press@yale.edu (U.S. office) or sales@yaleup.co.uk (U.K. office).

Set in Janson type by IDS Infotech, Ltd.
Printed in the United States of America.

Library of Congress Control Number: 2017937443
ISBN 978-0-300-22344-6 (hardcover : alk. paper)

A catalogue record for this book is available from the British Library.

This paper meets the requirements of ANSI/NISO Z39.48-1992 (Permanence of Paper).

10 9 8 7 6 5 4 3

To Inge

The gap between medieval Christianity's ruling principle and everyday life is the great pitfall of the Middle Ages. It is the problem that runs through Gibbon's history, which he dealt with by a delicately malicious levity, pricking at every turn what seemed to him the hypocrisy of the Christian ideal as opposed to natural human functioning. . . .

Chivalry, the dominant idea of the ruling class, left as great a gap between ideal and practice as religion. The ideal was a vision of order maintained by the warrior class and formulated in the image of the Round Table, nature's perfect shape. King Arthur's knights adventured for the right against dragons, enchanters, and wicked men, establishing order in a wild world. So their living counterparts were supposed, in theory, to serve as defenders of the Faith, upholders of justice, champions of the oppressed. In practice, they were themselves the oppressors, and by the 14th century the violence and lawlessness of men of the sword had become a major agency of disorder. When the gap between ideal and real becomes too wide, the system breaks down. Legend and story have always reflected this; in the Arthurian romances the Round Table is shattered from within. The sword is returned to the lake; the effort begins anew. Violent, destructive, greedy, fallible as he may be, man retains his vision of order and resumes his search.

—BARBARA TUCHMAN, *A Distant Mirror: The Calamitous 14th Century*

Contents

CONTENTS

Foreword

The Yale University Press series Politics and Culture begins
with the premise that self-government, the hallmark and glory
of the United States, the West, and an expanding number of
countries around the world, is ailing. Those who sense the
ailment cannot agree on what it is, much less how it is to be
treated; and that disagreement, only deepening as time passes,
is in fact part of the ailment. In the young twenty-first century,
liberal democracy, that system that marries majority rule with
individual rights, has entered a crisis of legitimacy. As practiced
in recent decades, and as an international ordering principle,
it has failed to deliver on its promises to growing, and increasingly mobilized and vocal, numbers of people.

The symptoms of this ailment are easy to observe: an
increasing skew in the distribution of wealth; decay in traditional institutions, from civic associations to labor unions to the
family; a loss of trust in authority—political, religious, scientific, journalistic—and among citizens themselves; growing

disillusionment with progress in effecting equal justice for all; above all, perhaps, the persistent and widening polarization between those who want increasingly open and experimental societies and those who want to conserve various traditional institutions and practices. The fragmentation not only continues but deepens. As people sort into new social and political tribes, electoral results confound and alarm experts and further widen polarization. W. B. Yeats's line "the center cannot hold" applies in our fractured societies as much as it did when he wrote it a century ago. In the age of Trump, it is not even clear where the center is or how we might rediscover and reoccupy it.

Patrick Deneen's *Why Liberalism Failed*, the second book in this series, locates the source of the legitimacy crisis in liberalism itself. By liberalism, Deneen has in mind not the narrow definition of popular American discourse, namely progressive big government or caring government (depending on your point of view). He means the broader conception familiar to political philosophers, the set of principles upon which liberal democracies the world over are built. *Why Liberalism Failed* pulls together a number of strands of discontent about liberalism today, strands found in academic, political, and popular discourse. The result is a bold and far-reaching critique of the root liberal assumption, associated with the Enlightenment philosopher Immanuel Kant, of individual autonomy. We use the "root" metaphor deliberately: Deneen's is a radical critique, arguing that liberalism needs not reform but retirement. The problem is not that liberalism has been hijacked but that its elevation of individual autonomy was wrong from the start, and the passage of decades has only made its error more evident.

Scholars have launched radical critiques of liberalism before. From the left have come broadsides from Marx and his progeny, including the Frankfurt School, and from postmodern thinkers such as Foucault. From the right have come attacks from Nietzsche, Schmitt, and traditionalists in the Catholic Church and other religious institutions. From a location difficult to pinpoint have come onslaughts from Milbank and Hauerwas. Such critiques inevitably provoke strong reactions from other scholars and intellectuals. Radical critiques are designed to do that—to disrupt the dominant discourse and challenge its routine absorption and redirection of critique, so that people will think more fundamentally about existing political, social, and economic institutions and practices.

Readers of all sorts will find that *Why Liberalism Failed* challenges not only their thinking but many of their most cherished assumptions about politics and our political order. Deneen's book is disruptive not only for the way it links social maladies to liberalism's first principles, but also because it is difficult to categorize along our conventional left-right spectrum. Much of what he writes will cheer social democrats and anger free-market advocates; much else will hearten traditionalists and alienate social progressives. Some of these readers nonetheless will be tempted to place the book in one or another familiar category, the better to manage and perhaps dismiss its critique. They should resist that temptation, which is itself a symptom of our polarized times and perhaps the chief reason why Deneen's argument is precisely the kind we most need to hear now.

James Davison Hunter
and John M. Owen IV, Series Editors

Preface

This book was completed three weeks before the 2016 presidential election. Its main arguments matured over the past decade, before Brexit or President Trump was even conceivable. My basic assumption was that the underpinnings of our inherited civilized order—norms learned in families, in communities, through religion and a supporting culture—would inevitably erode under the influence of the liberal social and political state. But I anticipated that liberalism would relentlessly continue replacing traditional cultural norms and practices with statist Band-Aids, even as a growing crisis of legitimacy would force its proponents to impose liberal ideology upon an increasingly recalcitrant populace. Liberalism would thus simultaneously "prevail" and fail by becoming more nakedly itself.

From that vantage, I hinted that such a political condition was ultimately untenable, and that the likely popular reaction to an increasingly oppressive liberal order might be forms of authoritarian *illiberalism* that would promise citizens power over those forces that no longer seemed under their control: government, economy, and the dissolution of social norms and unsettled ways of life. For liberals, this would prove the need for tighter enforcement of a liberal regime, but they would be blind to how this crisis of legitimacy had been created by liberalism itself. I did not suggest these conclusions expecting to see such a dynamic come to pass in my lifetime, and might have written a somewhat different book in light of recent events. However, I believe my original analysis still helps us understand the basic outlines of our moment, and avoids the excessively narrow focus that can come from too deep an immersion in headlines.

Today's widespread yearning for a strong leader, one with the will to take back popular control over liberalism's forms of bureaucratized government and globalized economy, comes after decades of liberal dismantling of cultural norms and political habits essential to self-governance. The breakdown of family, community, and religious norms and institutions, especially among those benefiting least from liberalism's advance, has not led liberalism's discontents to seek a restoration of those norms. That would take effort and sacrifice in a culture that now diminishes the value of both. Rather, many now look to deploy the statist powers of liberalism against its own ruling class. Meanwhile, huge energies are spent in mass protest rather than in self-legislation and deliberation, reflecting less a renewal of democratic governance than political fury and despair. Liberalism created the conditions, and the tools, for the ascent of its own worst nightmare, yet it lacks the self-knowledge to understand its own culpability.

While I end this volume by calling on political philosophers for help in finding a way out of the vise in which we now find ourselves—the mental grip of those revolutionary ideologies inaugurated in modernity first by liberalism itself—the better course lies not in any political revolution but in the patient encouragement of new forms of community that can serve as havens in our depersonalized political and economic order. As the Czech dissident Václav Havel wrote in "The Power of the Powerless": "A better system will not automatically ensure a better life. In fact, the opposite is true: only by creating a better life can a better system be developed."[1] Only a politics grounded in the experience of a *polis*—lives shared with a sense of common purpose, with obligations and gratitude arising from sorrows, hopes, and joys lived in generational time, and with the cultivation of capacities of trust and faith—can begin to take the place of our era's distrust, estrangement, hostility, and hatreds. As my teacher and friend Carey McWilliams wrote at the conclusion of one of his most penetrating essays, "strengthening [our shared] democratic life is a difficult, even daunting, task requiring sacrifice and patience more than dazzling exploits."[2] Sacrifice and patience are not the hallmarks of the age of statist individualism. But they will be needed in abundance for us to usher in a better, doubtless very different, time after liberalism.

Acknowledgments

This short book was written in a brief span—after several decades of reflection. My debts are therefore many, and in some cases the acknowledgment of my gratitude is long overdue.

The unpayable debts to the late Wilson Carey McWilliams, my friend and teacher, should be everywhere in evidence on these pages. He would have written a much better book on the travails of liberalism, but I would trade such a book for just one more conversation on the state of the world between sips of bourbon and laughter.

The first ideas of this book were conceived at Rutgers and Princeton, and I am thankful for generous interlocutors like George Kateb, Robert P. George, and the late Paul Sigmund. I am grateful to the James Madison Program in American Ideals and Institutions, and its associate director Brad Wilson, for a timely fellowship during 2008–9.

Many of these ideas matured during my years at Georgetown University. I am indebted to Joshua Mitchell, Father

James V. Schall, S.J., Father Stephen Fields, S.J., and two departed friends, Jean Bethke Elshtain and George Carey. I most gratefully acknowledge the friendship and support of Bill Mumma. I remain in awe of the many students who together made the Tocqueville Forum so special during its most glorious years.

At Notre Dame, our lives have been suffused with sustaining friendships. My gratitude to Phillip Muñoz, Susan Collins, John O'Callaghan, Sean and Christel Kelsey, Dave O'Connor, Philip Bess, John and Alicia Nagy, Francesca Murphy, John Betz, John Cavadini, Gerard Bradley, Rick and Nicole Garnett, Jeff Pojanowski, Martijn Cremers, Father Bill Miscamble, David Solomon, Carter Snead, Gladden Pappin, Dan Philpott, Mike Griffin, Anna and Michael Moreland, and Brad Gregory. I gratefully acknowledge the generosity of two vital programs at the University of Notre Dame, the Center for Ethics and Culture and the Tocqueville Program for Inquiry into Religion and Public Life, both which supported completion of this book. My thanks also to Mimi Teixeira, who assisted with preparation of the manuscript.

More friends than I can possibly acknowledge have helped me in countless ways, and I hope you find fruits of our conversations here, along with my deepest gratitude. My thanks to Chad Pecknold, Francis X. Maier, Rod Dreher, Bill McClay, Jeremy Beer (who suggested a version of the title), Mark Henrie, Jason Peters, Jeff Polet, Mark Mitchell, Brad Birzer, Phillip Blond, Cindy Searcy, Dan Mahoney, John Seery, Susan McWilliams, Brad Klingele, and Michael Hanby. I am grateful to Rusty Reno, David Mills, Dan McCarthy, John Leo, and Scott Stephens for publishing several early versions of parts of these chapters. I especially thank Steve Wrinn for his wise counsel and friendship over so many years.

I'm grateful to the Institute for the Advanced Studies on Culture at the University of Virginia, particularly James Davison Hunter and John Owen IV, who expressed early interest in this project. My thanks to Bill Frucht, who urged me to write short and so gamely championed the book at Yale University Press.

Shortly before the book went to press, two friends of long standing passed away, Benjamin Barber and Peter Lawler. I would that my teacher Ben and my valued interlocutor and friend Peter might have been able to read some fruits of our many conversations and debates. Their voices and ideas are here, and remain too in the many lives they touched. But still, I miss them both.

To my wife, Inge, and our children Francis, Adrian, and Alexandra, my heart is full and words fail.

And because so many years have passed since the intimations of this project began whispering to me, doubtless there are many owed my thanks whom I haven't named here. You know who you are. My deepest and abiding gratitude.

WHY LIBERALISM FAILED

Introduction: The End of Liberalism

A political philosophy conceived some 500 years ago, and put into effect at the birth of the United States nearly 250 years later, was a wager that political society could be grounded on a different footing. It conceived humans as rights-bearing individuals who could fashion and pursue for themselves their own version of the good life. Opportunities for liberty were best afforded by a limited government devoted to "securing rights," along with a free-market economic system that gave space for individual initiative and ambition. Political legitimacy was grounded on a shared belief in an originating "social contract" to which even newcomers could subscribe, ratified continuously by free and fair elections of responsive representatives. Limited but effective government, rule of law, an independent judiciary, responsive public officials, and free and fair elections were some of the hallmarks of this ascendant order and, by all evidence, wildly successful wager.

Today, some 70 percent of Americans believe that their country is moving in the wrong direction, and half the country thinks its best days are behind it. Most believe that their children will be less prosperous and have fewer opportunities than previous generations. Every institution of government shows declining levels of public trust by the citizenry, and deep cynicism toward politics is reflected in an uprising on all sides of the political spectrum against political and economic elites. Elections, once regarded as well-orchestrated performances meant to convey legitimacy to liberal democracy, are increasingly regarded as evidence of an impregnably rigged and corrupt system. It is evident to all that the political system is broken and social fabric is fraying, particularly as a growing gap increases between wealthy haves and left-behind have-nots, a hostile divide widens between faithful and secular peoples, and deep disagreement persists over America's role in the world. Wealthy Americans continue to gravitate to gated enclaves in and around select cities, while growing numbers of Christians compare our times to that of the late Roman Empire and ponder a fundamental withdrawal from wider American society into updated forms of Benedictine monastic communities. The signs of the times suggest that much is wrong with America. A growing chorus of voices even warn that we may be witnessing the end of the Republic unfolding before our eyes, with some yet-unnamed regime in the midst of taking its place.

Nearly every one of the promises that were made by the architects and creators of liberalism has been shattered. The liberal state expands to control nearly every aspect of life while citizens regard government as a distant and uncontrollable power, one that only extends their sense of powerlessness by relentlessly advancing the project of "globalization." The only rights that seem secure today belong to those with sufficient wealth and position to protect them, and their autonomy—including rights of property, the franchise and its concomitant control over representative institutions, religious liberty, free speech, and security in one's papers and abode—is increasingly compromised by legal intent or technological fait accompli. The economy favors a new "meritocracy" that perpetuates its advantages through generational succession, shored up by an educational system that relentlessly sifts winners from losers. A growing distance between liberalism's claims and its actuality increasingly spurs doubts about those claims rather than engendering trust that the gap will be narrowed.

Liberalism has failed—not because it fell short, but because it was true to itself. It has failed because it has succeeded. As liberalism has "become more fully itself," as its inner logic has become more evident and its self-contradictions manifest, it has generated pathologies that are at once deformations of its claims yet realizations of liberal ideology. A political philosophy that was launched to foster greater equity, defend a pluralist tapestry of different cultures and beliefs, protect human dignity, and, of course, expand liberty, in practice generates titanic inequality, enforces uniformity and homogeneity, fosters material and spiritual degradation, and undermines freedom. Its success can be measured by its achievement of the opposite of what we have believed it would achieve. Rather than seeing the accumulating catastrophe as evidence of our failure to live up to liberalism's ideals, we need rather to see clearly that the ruins it has produced are the signs of its very success. To call for the cures of liberalism's ills by applying more liberal measures is tantamount to throwing gas on a raging fire. It will only deepen our political, social, economic, and moral crisis.

This may be a moment for more than mere institutional tinkering. If indeed something more fundamental and transformative than "normal politics" is happening, then we are in the midst not just of a political realignment, characterized by the dying gasp of an old white working class and the lashing out of debt-burdened youth. We may rather be witnessing an increasingly systemic failure, due to the bankruptcy of its underlying political philosophy, of the political system we have largely taken for granted. The fabric of beliefs that gave rise to the nearly 250-year-old American constitutional experiment may be nearing an end. While a number of our Founding Fathers believed that they had lighted on a "new science of politics" that would resist the inevitable tendency of all regimes to decay and eventually die—even comparing the constitutional order to an entropy-defying perpetual motion device, "a machine that would go of itself"—we should rightly wonder whether America is not in the early days of its eternal life but rather approaching the end of the natural cycle of corruption and decay that limits the lifespan of all human creations.

This political philosophy has been for modern Americans like water for a fish, an encompassing political ecosystem in which we have swum, unaware of its existence. Liberalism is the first of the modern world's three great competitor political ideologies, and with the demise of fascism and communism, it is the only ideology still with a claim to viability. As ideology, liberalism was the first political architecture that proposed transforming all aspects of human life to conform to a preconceived political plan. We live in a society and increasingly a world that has been remade in the image of an ideology—the first nation founded by the explicit embrace of liberal philosophy, whose citizenry is shaped almost entirely by its commitments and vision.

But unlike the visibly authoritarian regimes that arose in dedication to advancing the ideologies of fascism and communism, liberalism is less visibly ideological and only surreptitiously remakes the world in its image. In contrast to its crueler competitor ideologies, liberalism is more insidious: as an ideology, it pretends to neutrality, claiming no preference and denying any intention of shaping the souls under its rule. It ingratiates by invitation to the easy liberties, diversions, and attractions of freedom, pleasure, and wealth. It makes itself invisible, much as a computer's operating system goes largely unseen—until it crashes. Liberalism becomes daily more visible precisely because its deformations are becoming too obvious to ignore. As Socrates tells us in Plato's *Republic*, most humans in most times and places occupy a cave, believing it to be a complete reality. What's most insidious about the cave that we occupy is that its walls are like the backdrops of old movie sets, promising seemingly endless vistas without constraints or limits, and thus our containment remains invisible to us.

Among the few iron laws of politics, few seem more unbreakable than the ultimate unsustainability of ideology in politics. Ideology fails for two reasons—first, because it is based on falsehood about human nature, and hence can't help but fail; and second, because as those falsehoods become more evident, the gap grows between what the ideology claims and the lived experience of human beings under its domain until the regime loses legitimacy. Either it enforces conformity to a lie it struggles to defend, or it collapses when the gap between claim and reality finally results in wholesale loss of belief among the populace. More often than not, one precedes the other.

Thus, even as liberalism has penetrated nearly every nation on earth, its vision of human liberty seems increasingly to be a taunt rather than a promise. Far from celebrating the utopic freedom at the "end of history" that seemed within grasp when the last competing ideology fell in 1989, humanity comprehensively shaped by liberalism is today burdened by the miseries of its successes. It pervasively finds itself to be caught in a trap of its own making, entangled in the very apparatus that was supposed to grant pure and unmitigated freedom.

We can see this today especially in four distinct but connected areas of our common life: politics and government, economics, education, and science and technology. In each of these domains, liberalism has transformed human institutions in the name of expanding liberty and increasing our mastery and control of our fates. And in each case, widespread anger and deepening discontent have arisen from the spreading realization that the vehicles of our liberation have become iron cages of our captivity.

POLITICS

Citizens of advanced liberal democracies are in near revolt against their own governments, the "establishment," and the politicians they have themselves selected as their leaders and representatives. Overwhelming majorities regard their governments as distant and unresponsive, captured by the wealthy, and ruling solely for the advantage of the powerful. At its inception, liberalism promised to displace an old aristocracy in the name of liberty; yet as it eliminates every vestige of an old order, the heirs of their hopeful antiaristocratic forebears regard its replacement as a new, perhaps even more pernicious, kind of aristocracy.

Liberalism was premised upon the limitation of government and the liberation of the individual from arbitrary political control. But growing numbers of citizens regard the government as an entity separate from their own will and control, not their creature and creation as promised by liberal philosophy. The "limited government" of liberalism today would provoke jealousy and amazement from tyrants of old, who could only dream of such extensive capacities for surveillance and control of movement, finances, and even deeds and thoughts. The liberties that liberalism was brought into being to protect—individual rights of conscience, religion, association, speech, and self-governance—are extensively compromised by the expansion of government activity into every area of life. Yet this expansion continues, largely as a response to people's felt loss of power over the trajectory of their lives in so many distinct spheres—economic and otherwise—leading to demands for further intervention by the one entity even nominally under their control. Our government readily complies, moving like a ratchet wrench, always in one direction, enlarging and expanding in response to civic grievances, ironically leading in turn to citizens' further experience of distance and powerlessness.

Citizens thus feel only tenuously connected to political representatives whose work was to "refine and enlarge" the public sentiment. Representatives in turn express their relative powerlessness in relation to a permanent bureaucracy staffed by career employees whose incentive is to maintain or enlarge their budgets and activity. More power accrues to the executive branch, which nominally controls the bureaucracy and through administrative rules can at least provide the appearance of responsiveness to a restive polity. Political rule by an increasingly unpopular legislature that theoretically derives its legitimacy from the people is replaced with commands and mandates of an executive whose office is achieved by massive influxes of lucre.[1] Liberalism claimed to replace arbitrary rule by distant and popularly unchosen leaders with responsive rule through elected public servants. Our electoral process today, however, appears more to be a Potemkin drama meant to convey the appearance of popular consent for a figure who will exercise incomparable arbitrary powers over domestic policy, international arrangements, and, especially, war-making.

Such a keenly felt distance and lack of control is not a condition to be solved by a better and more perfect liberalism—rather, this crisis of governance is the culmination of the liberal order. Liberalism proposed that occasional consent would suffice for the elevation of a leadership class composed of those of "fit characters"—namely those, in the incomparable words of Alexander Hamilton, concerned with "commerce, finance, negotiation and war, all the objects which have charms for minds governed by that passion." The system's architects intended to encourage a focus on private concerns among the citizenry—a *res idiotica* that they called a "republic." If there is difficulty "keeping it," a republic cannot survive in the absence of "public things." The belief that liberalism could achieve *modus vivendi* by encouraging privatism has culminated in the nearly complete disassociation of the governing class and a citizenry without a *cives*.

ECONOMICS

Civic unhappiness is mirrored in economic discontent. Citizens are more likely to be called "consumers," yet the liberty to buy every imaginable consumer good does little to assuage the widespread economic anxiety and discontent over waxing inequality—indeed, the assumption by economic leaders seems to be that increased purchasing power of cheap goods will compensate for the absence of economic security and the division of the world into generational winners and losers. There has always been, and probably always will be, economic inequality, but few civilizations appear to have so extensively perfected the separation of winners from losers or created such a massive apparatus to winnow those who will succeed from those who will fail. Marx once argued that the greatest source of economic discontent was not necessarily inequality but alienation—the separation of worker from product and the attendant loss of any connection with the goal and object of one's efforts. Today's economy not only maintains and extends this alienation but adds a profound new form of geographic alienation, the physical separation of beneficiaries of the globalized economy from those left behind. This leads the economic winners to combine lamentations of economic inequality with sotto voce denunciations of the backward views of those who condemn globalization's course. The losers, meanwhile, are consoled with the reminder that they are wealthy beyond compare to even the wealthiest aristocrats of an earlier age. Material comforts are a ready salve for the discontents of the soul.

As the reactions in the urban centers to the outcome of the Brexit vote and the election of Donald J. Trump evince, those same leaders are shocked that the terms of the social contract appear not to be acceptable to Walmart shoppers. Still, nothing can finally be done, for globalization is an inevitable process, unstoppable by any individual or nation. Whatever one thinks of economic integration, standardization, and homogenization, it is pointless to entertain thoughts of alternatives. One of globalization's cheerleaders, Thomas Friedman, has defined it in just such terms of inevitability:

> It is the inevitable integration of markets, nation-states and technologies to a degree never witnessed before—in a way that is enabling individuals, corporations and nation-states to reach around the world farther, faster, deeper and cheaper than ever before and in a way that is enabling the world to reach into individuals, corporations and nation-states farther, faster, deeper, cheaper than ever before.[2]

Whether people want the world "reaching into" individuals, corporations, and nation states is not a matter for discussion, for the process cannot be stopped. The economic system that simultaneously is both liberalism's handmaiden and its engine, like a Frankenstein monster, takes on a life of its own, and its processes and logic can no longer be controlled by people purportedly enjoying the greatest freedom in history. The wages of freedom are bondage to economic inevitability.

EDUCATION

The rising generation is indoctrinated to embrace an economic and political system they distinctly fear, filling them with cynicism toward their future and their participation in maintaining an order they cannot avoid but which they neither believe in nor trust. Far from feeling themselves to constitute the most liberated and autonomous generation in history, young adults believe less in their task at hand than Sisyphus rolling the boulder up the mountainside. They accede in the duties demanded of them by their elders, but without joy or love—only with a keen sense of having no other choice. Their overwhelming response to their lot—expressed in countless comments they have offered to me over the years describing their experience and expectations of their own education—is one of entrapment and "no exit," of being cynical participants in a system that ruthlessly produces winners and losers even as it demands that they understand this system to be a vehicle of "social justice." One can hardly be surprised that even the "winners" admit during frank moments that they are both swindlers and swindled. As one student described the lot of her generation to me:

> We are meritocrats out of a survivalist instinct. If we do not race to the very top, the only remaining option is a bottomless

pit of failure. To simply work hard and get decent grades doesn't cut it anymore if you believe there are only two options: the very top or rock bottom. It is a classic prisoner's dilemma: to sit around for 2–3 hours at the dining hall "shooting the breeze," or to spend time engaged in intellectual conversation in moral and philosophical issues, or to go on a date all detract from time we could be spending on getting to the top and, thus, will leave us worse off relative to everyone else. . . . Because we view humanity—and thus its institutions—as corrupt and self-ish, the only person we can rely upon is our self. The only way we can avoid failure, being let down, and ultimately succumb-ing to the chaotic world around us, therefore, is to have the means (financial security) to rely only upon ourselves.[3]

Advanced liberalism is eliminating liberal education with keen intent and ferocity, finding it impractical both ideologi-cally and economically. Students are taught by most of their humanities and social science professors that the only remain-ing political matter at hand is to equalize respect and dignity accorded to all people, even as those institutions are mills for sifting the economically viable from those who will be mocked for their backward views on trade, immigration, nationhood, and religious beliefs. The near unanimity of political views rep-resented on college campuses is echoed by the omnipresent belief that an education must be economically practical, culmi-nating in a high-paying job in a city populated by like-minded college graduates who will continue to reinforce their keen outrage over inequality while enjoying its bounteous fruits. Universities scramble to provide practical "learning outcomes," either by introducing a raft of new programs aimed to make students immediately employable or by rebranding and reori-enting existing studies to tout their economic relevance. There is simply *no choice* to do otherwise in a globalizing, economically competitive world. Few remark upon the fact that this locution becomes ever more common in advanced liberalism, the regime that was supposed to ensure endless free choice.

At the moment of liberalism's culmination, then, we see the headlong evacuation of the liberal arts. The liberal arts were long understood to be the essential form of education for a free people, especially citizens who aspired to self-government. The emphasis on the great texts—which were great not only or even because they were old but because they contained hard-won lessons on how humans learn to be free, especially free from the tyranny of their insatiable desires—has been jettisoned in favor of what was once considered "servile education," an education concerned exclusively with money making and a life of work, and hence reserved for those who did not enjoy the title of "citizen." Today's liberals condemn a regime that once separated freeman from serf, master from slave, citizen from servant, but even as we have ascended to the summit of moral superiority over our benighted forebears by proclaiming everyone free, we have almost exclusively adopted the educational form that was reserved for those who were deprived of freedom. And yet in the midst of our glorious freedom, we don't think to ask why we no longer have the luxury of an education whose very name—liberal arts—indicates its fundamental support for the cultivation of the free person.

SCIENCE AND TECHNOLOGY

Today's students are especially encouraged to study a discipline that is useful, particularly those related to STEM—science, technology, engineering, and mathematics. Liberalism's tools for liberating humanity from various forms of bondage were especially to be achieved through transformations in politics, namely the representative system that today seems out of our control; economics, particularly market capitalism, whose globalizing logic cannot be resisted; and science and technology, arguably the greatest source of our liberation and simultaneously the reason for our imperiled environment, the deformations wrought by our own technologies on our personhood, and deep anxiety over our inability to control our own innovations. The modern scientific project of human liberation from the tyranny of nature has been framed as an effort to "master" or "control" nature, or as a "war" against nature in which its study would provide the tools for its subjugation at the hands of humans. Francis Bacon—who rejected classical arguments that learning aimed at the virtues of wisdom, prudence, and justice, arguing instead that "knowledge is power"—compared nature to a prisoner who, under torture, might be compelled to reveal her long-withheld secrets.

Even if we do not speak in these terms any more, the modern scientific project now dominates what we regard as useful and rewarding inquiry. Yet nature seems not to have surrendered. As the farmer and author Wendell Berry has written, if modern science and technology were conceived as a "war against nature," then "it is a war in every sense—nature is fighting us as much as we are fighting it. And . . . it appears that we are losing."[4] Many elements of what we today call our environmental crisis—climate change, resource depletion, groundwater contamination and scarcity, species extinction— are signs of battles won but a war being lost. Today we are accustomed to arguing that we should follow the science in an issue such as climate change, ignoring that our crisis is the result of long-standing triumphs of science and technology in which "following science" was tantamount to civilizational progress. Our carbon-saturated world is the hangover of a 150-year party in which, until the very end, we believed we had achieved the dream of liberation from nature's constraints. We still hold the incoherent view that science can liberate us from limits while solving the attendant consequences of that project.

Meanwhile, we are increasingly shaped by technology that promises liberation from limits of place, time, and even identity. The computer in every person's pocket has been shown to change the structure of our minds, turning us into different creatures, conforming us to the demands and nature of a technology that is supposed to allow expression of our true selves.[5] How many of us can sit for an hour reading a book or simply thinking or meditating without an addict's longing for just a hit of the cell phone, that craving that won't allow us to think or concentrate or reflect until we've had our hit? This same technology that is supposed to connect us more extensively and intimately is making us more lonely, more apart.[6] Devices increasingly replace humans in the workplace, apparently granting us liberty but making us our technology's ward and helpmeet. And advances in the manipulation of nature inevitably raise the possibility of remaking humanity itself, potentially pitting Humanity 2.0 against those who refuse or can't afford to shuck version 1.0.[7]

What is supposed to allow us to transform our world is instead transforming us, making us into creatures to which many, if not most of us, have not given our "consent." It is making us ever more into the creatures that liberalism supposed was our nature in that "state of nature" that existed before the coming of civilization, law, and government. Ironically, but perhaps not coincidentally, the political project of liberalism is shaping us into the creatures of its prehistorical fantasy, which in fact required the combined massive apparatus of the modern state, economy, education system, and science and technology to make us into: increasingly separate, autonomous, nonrelational selves replete with rights and defined by our liberty, but insecure, powerless, afraid, and alone.

Liberalism's success today is most visible in the gathering signs of its failure. It has remade the world in its image, especially through the realms of politics, economics, education, science, and technology, all aimed at achieving supreme and complete freedom through the liberation of the individual from particular places, relationships, memberships, and even identities—unless they have been chosen, are worn lightly, and can be revised or abandoned at will. The autonomous self is thus subject to the sovereign trajectory of the very forces today that are embraced as the tools of our liberation. Yet our liberation renders us incapable of resisting these defining forces—the promise of freedom results in thralldom to inevitabilities to which we have no choice but to submit.

These tools were deployed to liberate individuals from the "givenness" of their condition, especially through "depersonalization" and "abstraction," liberalism's vision of liberty from particular duties, obligations, debts, and relationships. These ends have been achieved through the depersonalization and abstraction advanced via two main entities—the state and the market. Yet while they have worked together in a pincer movement to render us ever more naked as individuals, our political debates mask this alliance by claiming that allegiance to one of these forces will save us from the depredations of the other. Our main political choices come down to which depersonalized mechanism will purportedly advance our freedom and security—the space of the market, which collects our billions upon billions of choices to provide for our wants and needs without demanding from us any specific thought or intention about the wants and needs of others; or the liberal state, which establishes depersonalized procedures and mechanisms for the wants and needs of others that remain insufficiently addressed by the market.

Thus the insistent demand that we choose between protection of individual liberty and expansion of state activity masks the true relation between the state and market: that they grow constantly and necessarily together. Statism enables individualism, individualism demands statism. For all the claims about electoral transformations—for "Hope and Change" or "Making America Great Again"—two facts are naggingly apparent: modern liberalism proceeds by making us both more individualist and more statist. This is not because one party advances individualism without cutting back on statism while the other does the opposite; rather, both move simultaneously in tune with our deepest philosophic premises.

Claiming to liberate the individual from embedded cultures, traditions, places, and relationships, liberalism has homogenized the world in its image—ironically, often fueled by claims of "multiculturalism" or, today, "diversity." Having successfully disembedded us from relationships that once made claims upon us but also informed our conception of selfhood, our sense of ourselves as citizens sharing a common fate and as economic actors sharing a common world, liberalism has left the individual exposed to the tools of liberation— leaving us in a weakened state in which the domains of life that were supposed to liberate us are completely beyond our control or governance. This suggests that all along, the individual was the "tool" of the liberal system, not—as was believed—vice versa.

The most challenging step we must take is a rejection of the belief that the ailments of liberal society can be fixed by realizing liberalism. The only path to liberation from the inevitabilities and ungovernable forces that liberalism imposes is liberation from liberalism itself. Both main political options of our age must be understood as different sides of the same counterfeit coin. Neither Progressivism's faith that liberalism will be realized when we move forward toward the realization of liberalism's promise nor Conservatism's tale that American greatness will be restored when we reclaim the governing philosophy of our Constitution offers any real alternative to liberalism's advance.

The past can instruct, but there can be no return and no "restoration." Liberalism has ruthlessly drawn down a reservoir of both material and moral resources that it cannot replenish. Its successes were always blank checks written against a future it trusted it could repair. Conservatism rightly observes that progressivism's destination is a dead end, and progressivism rightly decries conservatism's nostalgia for a time that cannot be restored. Conservatives and progressives alike have advanced liberalism's project, and neither as constituted today can provide the new way forward that must be discerned outside our rutted path.

Nor does reflecting upon what follows liberalism's self-destruction imply that we must simply devise its opposite, or deny what was of great and enduring value in the achievements of liberalism. Liberalism's appeal lies in its continuities with the deepest commitments of the Western political tradition, particularly efforts to secure liberty and human dignity through the constraint of tyranny, arbitrary rule, and oppression. In this regard, liberalism is rightly considered to be based on essential political commitments that were developed over centuries in classical and Christian thought and practice. Yet liberalism's innovations—ones that its architects believed would more firmly secure human liberty and dignity—which consisted especially of a redefinition of the ideal of liberty and a reconception of human nature, have undermined the realization of its stated commitments. Moving beyond liberalism is not to discard some of liberalism's main commitments—especially those deepest longings of the West, political liberty and human dignity—but to reject the false turn it made in its imposition of an ideological remaking of the world in the image of a false anthropology.

A rejection of the world's first and last remaining ideology does not entail its replacement with a new and doubtless not very different ideology. Political revolution to overturn a revolutionary order would produce only disorder and misery. A better course will consist in smaller, local forms of resistance:

practices more than theories, the building of resilient new cultures against the anticulture of liberalism.

When Alexis de Tocqueville visited America in the early decades of the nineteenth century, he observed that Americans tended to act differently from and better than their individualistic and selfish ideology. "They do more honor to their philosophy than to themselves," he wrote. What's needed now is not to perfect our philosophy any further but to again do more honor to ourselves. Out of the fostering of new and better selves, porously invested in the fate of other selves—through the cultivation of cultures of community, care, self-sacrifice, and small-scale democracy—a better practice might arise, and from it, ultimately, perhaps a better theory than the failing project of liberalism.

CHAPTER ONE

Unsustainable Liberalism

T HE deepest commitment of liberalism is expressed by the name itself: liberty. Liberalism has proven both attractive and resilient because of this core commitment to the longing for human freedom so deeply embedded in the human soul. Liberalism's historical rise and global attraction are hardly accidental; it has appealed especially to people subject to arbitrary rule, unjust inequality, and pervasive poverty. No other political philosophy had proven in practice that it could fuel prosperity, provide relative political stability, and foster individual liberty with such regularity and predictability. There were plausible grounds why, in 1989, Francis Fukuyama could declare that the long debate over ideal regimes had ended, and that liberalism was the end station of History.

Liberalism did not, of course, discover or invent the human longing for liberty: the word *libertas* is of ancient origin, and its defense and realization have been a primary goal from the first forays into political philosophy in ancient Greece and Rome. The foundational texts of the Western political tradition focused especially on the question how to constrain the impulse to and assertions of tyranny, and characteristically settled upon the cultivation of virtue and self-rule as the key correctives to the tyrannical temptation. The Greeks especially regarded self-government as a continuity from the individual to the polity, with the realization of either only possible if the virtues of temperance, wisdom, moderation, and justice were to be mutually sustained and fostered. Self-governance in the city was possible only if the virtue of self-governance governed the souls of citizens; and self-governance of individuals could be realized only in a city that understood that citizenship itself was a kind of ongoing habituation in virtue, through both law and custom. Greek philosophy stressed *paideia*, or education in virtue, as a primary path to forestalling the establishment of tyranny and protecting liberty of citizens, yet these conclusions coexisted (if at times at least uneasily) with justifications of inequality exemplified not only in calls for rule by a wise ruler of a class of rulers, but in the pervasiveness of slavery.

The Roman and then medieval Christian philosophical traditions retained the Greek emphasis upon the cultivation of virtue as a central defense against tyranny, but also developed institutional forms that sought to check the power of leaders while (to varying degrees) opening routes to informal and sometimes formal expression of popular opinion in political rule. Many of the institutional forms of government that we today associate with liberalism were at least initially conceived and developed over long centuries preceding the modern age, including constitutionalism, separation of powers, separate spheres of church and state, rights and protections against arbitrary rule, federalism, rule of law, and limited government.[1] Protection of rights of individuals and the belief in inviolable human dignity, if not always consistently recognized and practiced, were nevertheless philosophical achievements of premodern medieval Europe. Some scholars regard liberalism simply as the natural development, and indeed the culmination, of protoliberal thinking and achievements of this long period of development, and not as any sort of radical break from premodernity.[2]

While this claim is worthy of respectful consideration, given readily evident continuities, nevertheless contesting claims that a significant break occurred between modernity and premodernity—specifically that a novel political philosophy arose in distinction to premodern forebears—has considerable warrant. Indeed, the very institutional and even semantic continuities between classical and Christian premodernity and the modern period that eventuates in the rise of liberalism can be deceptive. The achievement of liberalism was not simply a wholesale rejection of its precedents, but in many cases attained its ends by redefining shared words and concepts and, through that redefinition, colonizing existing institutions with fundamentally different anthropological assumptions.

Liberty was fundamentally reconceived, even if the word was retained. Liberty had long been believed to be the condition of self-rule that forestalled tyranny, within both the polity and the individual soul. Liberty was thus thought to involve discipline and training in self-limitation of desires, and corresponding social and political arrangements that sought to inculcate corresponding virtues that fostered the arts of self-government. Classical and Christian political thought was self-admittedly more "art" than "science": it relied extensively on the fortunate appearance of inspiring founding figures and statesmen who could uphold political and social self-reinforcing virtuous cycles, and acknowledged the likelihood of decay and corruption as an inevitable feature of any human institution.

A signal hallmark of modernity was the rejection of this long-standing view of politics. Social and political arrange-ments came to be regarded as simultaneously ineffectual and undesirable. The roots of liberalism lay in efforts to overturn a variety of anthropological assumptions and social norms that had come to be believed as sources of pathology—name-ly, fonts of conflict as well as obstacles to individual liberty. The foundations of liberalism were laid by a series of thinkers whose central aim was to disassemble what they concluded were irrational religious and social norms in the pursuit of civil peace that might in turn foster stability and prosperity, and eventually individual liberty of conscience and action.

Three main efforts undergirded this revolution in thought and practice. First, politics would be based upon reliability of "the low" rather than aspiration to "the high." The classical and Christian effort to foster virtue was rejected as both pa-ternalistic and ineffectual, prone to abuse and unreliability. It was Machiavelli who broke with the classical and Christian aspiration to temper the tyrannical temptation through an education in virtue, scoring the premodern philosophic tradi-tion as an unbroken series of unrealistic and unreliable fanta-sies of "imaginary republics and principalities that have never existed in practice and never could; for the gap between how people actually behave and how they ought to behave is so great that anyone who ignores everyday reality in order to live up to an ideal will soon discover that he has been taught how to destroy himself, not how to preserve himself."[3] Rather than promoting unrealistic standards for behavior—especially self-limitation—that could at best be unreliably achieved, Machiavelli proposed grounding a political philosophy upon readily observable human behaviors of pride, selfishness, greed, and the quest for glory. He argued further that liberty and political security were better achieved by pitting different domestic classes against one another, encouraging each to limit the others through "ferocious conflict" in the protection of their particular interests rather than by lofty appeals to a "common good" and political concord. By acknowledging ineradicable human selfishness and the desire for material goods, one might conceive of ways to harness those motivations rather than seeking to moderate or limit those desires.

Second, the classical and Christian emphasis upon virtue and the cultivation of self-limitation and self-rule relied upon reinforcing norms and social structures arrayed extensively throughout political, social, religious, economic, and familial life. What were viewed as the essential supports for a training in virtue—and hence, preconditions for liberty from tyranny—came to be viewed as sources of oppression, arbitrariness, and limitation. Descartes and Hobbes in turn argued that the rule of irrational custom and unexamined tradition—especially religious belief and practice—was a source of arbitrary governance and unproductive internecine conflicts, and thus an obstacle to a stable and prosperous regime. Each proposed remediating the presence of custom and tradition by introducing "thought experiments" that reduced people to their natural essence—conceptually stripping humans of accidental attributes that obscured from us our true nature—so that philosophy and politics could be based upon a reasoned and reflective footing. Both expressed confidence in a more individualistic rationality that could replace long-standing social norms and customs as guides for action, and each believed that potential deviations from rationality could be corrected by the legal prohibitions and sanctions of a centralized political state.

Third, if political foundations and social norms required correctives to establish stability and predictability, and (eventually) to enlarge the realm of individual freedom, the human subjection to the dominion and limits of nature needed also to be overcome. A "new science of politics" was to be accompanied by a new *natural* science—in particular, a science that would seek practical applications meant to give humans a chance in the war against nature. Hobbes's employer, Francis Bacon, encouraged a new form of natural philosophy that would increase human empire over the natural world, providing for "relief of the human estate" through the expansion of useful applications of human knowledge.[4] A revolution in modern science thus called as well for overturning such philosophical traditions as Stoicism and Christian emphasis upon "acceptance" in favor of belief in an expanding and potentially limitless human capacity to control circumstance and effect human desires upon the world.

While none of these thinkers was a liberal, given their respective reservations regarding popular rule, their revolutionary reconception of politics, society, science, and nature laid the foundation of modern liberalism. A succession of thinkers in subsequent decades and centuries were to build upon these three basic revolutions of thought, redefining liberty as the liberation of humans from established authority, emancipation from arbitrary culture and tradition, and the expansion of human power and dominion over nature through advancing scientific discovery and economic prosperity. Liberalism's ascent and triumph required sustained efforts to undermine the classical and Christian understanding of liberty, the disassembling of widespread norms, traditions, and practices, and perhaps above all the reconceptualization of primacy of the individual defined in isolation from arbitrary accidents of birth, with the state as the main protector of individual rights and liberty.

The liberal adoption of these revolutions in thought and practice constituted a titanic wager that a wholly new understanding of liberty could be pursued and realized by overturning preceding philosophic tradition and religious and social norms, and by introducing a new relationship between humans and nature. What has become the literal "Whig" interpretation of political history widely holds that this wager has been an uncontested success. The advent of liberalism marks the end of a benighted age, the liberation of humanity from darkness, the overcoming of oppression and arbitrary inequality, the descent of monarchy and aristocracy, the advance of prosperity and modern technology, and the advent of an age of nearly unbroken progress. Liberalism is credited with the cessation of religious war, the opening of an age of tolerance and equality, the expanding spheres of personal opportunity and social interaction that today culminate in globalization, and the ongoing victories over sexism, racism, colonialism, heteronormativity, and a host of other unacceptable prejudices that divide, demean, and segregate.

Liberalism's victory was declared to be unqualified and complete in 1989 in the seminal article "The End of History" by Francis Fukuyama, written following the collapse of the last competing ideological opponent.[5] Fukuyama held that liberalism had proved itself the sole legitimate regime on the basis that it had withstood all challengers and defeated all competitors and further, that it *worked* because it accorded with human nature. A wager that was some five centuries in the making, and had been first instantiated as a political experiment by the Founders of the American liberal republic exactly two hundred years before Fukuyama's bold claim, had panned out with unprecedented clarity in the often muddled and contested realm of political philosophy and practice.

A main result of the widespread view that liberalism's triumph is complete and uncontested—indeed, that rival claims are no longer regarded as worthy of consideration—is a conclusion within the liberal order that various ills that infect the body politic as well as the civil and private spheres are either remnants of insufficiently realized liberalism or happenstance problems that are subject to policy or technological fix within the liberal horizon. Liberalism's own success makes it difficult to sustain reflection on the likelihood that the greatest current threat to liberalism lies not outside and beyond liberalism but within it. The potency of this threat arises from the fundamental nature of liberalism, from what are thought to be its very strengths—especially its faith in its ability of self-correction and its belief in progress and continual improvement—which make it largely impervious to discerning its deepest weaknesses and even self-inflicted decline. No matter our contemporary malady, there is no challenge that can't be fixed by a more perfect application of liberal solutions.

These maladies include the corrosive social and civic effects of self-interest—a disease that arises from the cure of overcoming the ancient reliance upon virtue. Not only is this malady increasingly manifest in all social interactions and institutions, but it infiltrates liberal politics. Undermining any appeal to common good, it induces a zero-sum mentality that becomes nationalized polarization for a citizenry that is increasingly driven by private and largely material concerns. Similarly, the "cure" by which individuals could be liberated from authoritative cultures generates social anomie that requires expansion of legal redress, police proscriptions, and expanded surveillance. For instance, because social norms and decencies have deteriorated and an emphasis on character was rejected as paternalistic and oppressive, a growing number of the nation's school districts now deploy surveillance cameras in schools, anonymous oversight triggering post-facto punishment. The cure of human mastery of nature is producing consequences that suggest such mastery is at best temporary and finally illusory: ecological costs of burning of fossil fuels, limits of unlimited application of antibiotics, political fallout from displacement of workforce by technology, and so forth. Among the greatest challenges facing humanity is the ability to survive progress.

Perhaps above all, liberalism has drawn down on a preliberal inheritance and resources that at once sustained liberalism but which it cannot replenish. The loosening of social bonds in nearly every aspect of life—familial, neighborly, communal, religious, even national—reflects the advancing logic of liberalism and is the source of its deepest instability. The increased focus upon, and intensifying political battles over, the role of centralized national and even international governments is at once the consequence of liberalism's move toward homogenization and one of the indications of its fragility. The global market displaces a variety of economic subcultures, enforcing a relentless logic of impersonal transactions that have led to a crisis of capitalism and the specter of its own unraveling. Battles in policy areas such as education and health care—in which either the state or the market is proposed as providing the resolution—reflect the weakening of forms of care that drew on more local commitments and devotions that neither the state nor market can hope to replicate or replace. The triumphant march of liberalism has succeeded in at once drawing down the social and natural resources that liberalism did not create and cannot replenish, but which sustained liberalism even as its advance eroded its own unacknowledged foundations.

Liberalism has been a wager that it can produce more benefits than the costs it would amass, all the while rendering liberal humanity widely insensate to the fact that the mounting costs are the result of those touted benefits. Thus most today view this wager as a settled bet, a question whose outcome is no longer in question. Yet the gathering evidence, once seen clearly as not circumstantially generated but arising directly from liberalism's fruition, reveals that the bookie's collector is knocking upon the door. While we have been slow to realize that the odds were in favor of the house, the damning evidence arising from liberalism's very success affirms that only blinkered ideology can conceal liberalism's unsustainability.

The strictly legal and political arrangements of modern constitutionalism do not per se constitute a liberal regime, but they are animated by two foundational beliefs. Liberalism is most fundamentally constituted by a pair of deeper anthropological assumptions that give liberal institutions a particular orientation and cast: 1) anthropological individualism and the voluntarist conception of choice, and 2) human separation from and opposition to nature. These two revolutions in the understanding of human nature and society constitute "liberalism" inasmuch as they introduce a radically new definition of "liberty."

LIBERAL VOLUNTARISM

The first revolution, and the most basic and distinctive aspect of liberalism, is to base politics upon the idea of voluntarism—the unfettered and autonomous choice of individuals. This argument was first articulated in the protoliberal defense of monarchy by Thomas Hobbes. According to Hobbes, human beings exist by nature in a state of radical independence and autonomy. Recognizing the fragility of a condition in which life in such a state is "nasty, brutish, and short," they employ their rational self-interest to sacrifice most of their natural rights in order to secure the protection and security of a sovereign. Legitimacy is conferred by consent.

The state is created to restrain the external actions of individuals and legally restricts the potentially destructive activity of radically separate human beings. Law is a set of practical restraints upon self-interested individuals; Hobbes does not assume the existence of self-restraint born of mutual concern. As he writes in *Leviathan*, law is comparable to hedges, "not to stop travelers, but to keep them in the way"; that is, law restrains people's natural tendency to act on "impetuous desires, rashness or indiscretion," and thus always acts as an external constraint upon our natural liberty.[6] By contrast, liberty persists "where there is silence of the law," limited only insofar as the "authorized" rules of the state are explicit.[7] Only the state can limit our natural liberty: the state is the sole creator and enforcer of positive law, and it even determines legitimate and illegitimate expressions of religious belief. The state is charged with maintaining social stability and preventing a return to natural anarchy; in so doing, it "secures" our natural rights.

Human beings are thus, by nature, nonrelational creatures, separate and autonomous. Liberalism begins a project by which the legitimacy of all human relationships—beginning with, but not limited to, political bonds—becomes increasingly dependent on whether those relationships have been chosen, and chosen on the basis of their service to rational self-interest.

As Hobbes's philosophical successor John Locke understood, voluntarist logic ultimately affects all relationships, including familial ones. Locke—the first philosopher of liberalism—on the one hand acknowledges in his *Second Treatise of Government* that the duties of parents to raise children and the corresponding duties of children to obey spring from the commandment "Honor thy father and mother," but he further claims that every child must ultimately subject his inheritance to the logic of consent, and thus begin (evoking the origin of human society) in a version of the State of Nature in which we act as autonomous choosing individuals. "For every *Man's Children* being by Nature as *free* as himself, or any of his Ancestors ever were, may, whilst they are in that Freedom, choose what Society they will join themselves to, what Common-wealths they will put themselves under. But if they will enjoy the *Inheritance* of their Ancestors, they must take it on the same terms their Ancestors had it, and submit to all the Conditions annex'd to such a Possession."[8] Even those who adopt the inheritance of their parents in every regard do so only through the logic of consent, even if it is tacit.

Even marriage, Locke holds, is finally to be understood as a contract whose conditions are temporary and subject to revision, particularly once the child-rearing duties are completed. If this encompassing logic of choice applies to the most elemental family relationships, then it applies all the more to the looser ties that bind people to other institutions and associations, in which membership is subject to constant monitoring and assessment of whether it benefits or unduly burdens any person's individual rights.

This is not to suggest that a preliberal era dismissed the idea of individual free choice. Among other significant ways that preliberal Christianity contributed to an expansion of human choice was to transform the idea of marriage from an institution based upon familial and property considerations to a choice made by consenting individuals on the basis of sacramental love. What was new is that the default basis for evaluating institutions, society, affiliations, memberships, and even personal relationships became dominated by considerations of individual choice based on the calculation of individual self-interest, and without broader consideration of the impact of one's choices upon the community, one's obligations to the created order, and ultimately to God.

Liberalism began with the explicit assertion that it merely describes our political, social, and private decision making. Yet it was implicitly constituted as a normative project: what it presented as a description of human voluntarism in fact had to displace a very different form of human self-understanding and experience. In effect, liberal theory sought to educate people to think differently about themselves and their relationships. Liberalism often claims neutrality about the choices people make in liberal society; it is the defender of "Right," not any particular conception of the "Good."

Yet it is not neutral about the basis on which people make their decisions. In the same way that courses in economics claim merely to describe human beings as utility-maximizing individual actors, but in fact influence students to act more selfishly, so liberalism teaches a people to hedge commitments and adopt flexible relationships and bonds. Not only are all political and economic relationships seen as fungible and subject to constant redefinition, so are *all* relationships—to place, to neighborhood, to nation, to family, and to religion. Liberalism encourages loose connections.

THE WAR AGAINST NATURE

The second revolution, and the second anthropological assumption that constitutes liberalism, is less visibly political.

Premodern political thought—particularly that informed by an Aristotelian understanding of natural science—understood the human creature as part of a comprehensive natural order. Humans were understood to have a *telos*, a fixed end, given by nature and unalterable. Human nature was continuous with the order of the natural world, and thus humanity was required to conform both to its own nature and, in a broader sense, to the natural order of which it was a part. Human beings could freely act against their own nature and the natural order, but such actions deformed them and harmed the good of human beings and the world. Aristotle's *Ethics* and Aquinas's *Summa Theologiae* are alike efforts to delineate the limits that nature—natural law—places upon human beings. Each seeks to educate man about how best to live within those limits through the practice of virtues, to achieve a condition of human flourishing.

Liberal philosophy rejected this requirement of human self-limitation. It displaced first the idea of a natural order to which humanity is subject and later the notion of human nature itself. Liberalism inaugurated a transformation in the natural and human sciences and humanity's relationship to the natural world. The first wave of this revolution—inaugurated by early-modern thinkers dating back to the Renaissance—insisted that man should employ natural science and a transformed economic system to seek mastery of nature. The second wave—developed largely by various historicist schools of thought, especially in the nineteenth century—replaced belief in the idea of a fixed human nature with belief in human "plasticity" and capacity for moral progress. These two iterations of liberalism—often labeled "conservative" and "progressive"—

contend today for ascendance, but we do better to understand their deep interconnection.

The protoliberal thinker who ushered in the first wave of liberalism's transformation was Francis Bacon. Like Hobbes (who was Bacon's secretary), he attacked the ancient Aristotelian and Thomistic understanding of nature and natural law and argued for the human capacity to "master" or "control" nature—even reversing the effects of the Fall, including even the possibility of overcoming human mortality.[9]

Liberalism became closely bound up with this new orientation of the natural sciences, and it embraced and advanced as well an economic system—market-based free enterprise—that similarly promoted human use, conquest, and mastery of the natural world. Early-modern liberalism held the view that *human* nature was unchangeable—human beings were, by nature, self-interested creatures whose base impulses could be harnessed but not fundamentally altered. But this self-interested, possessive aspect of our nature could, if usefully harnessed, promote an economic and scientific system that increased human freedom through the capacity of human beings to exert mastery over natural phenomena.

The second wave of this revolution begins as an explicit criticism of this view of humanity. Thinkers ranging from Rousseau to Marx, from Mill to Dewey, and from Richard Rorty to contemporary "transhumanists" reject the idea that human nature is fixed. They adopt the first-wave theorists' idea that nature is subject to human conquest and apply it to human nature itself.

First-wave liberals are today represented by "conservatives," who stress the need for scientific and economic mastery of nature but stop short of extending this project to human nature. They support nearly any utilitarian use of the world for economic ends but oppose most forms of biotechnological "enhancement." Second-wave liberals increasingly approve nearly any technical means of liberating humans from the biological nature of our own bodies. Today's political debates occur largely and almost exclusively between these two varieties of liberals. Neither side confronts the fundamentally alternative understanding of human nature and the human relationship to nature defended by the preliberal tradition.

Liberalism is thus not merely, as is often portrayed, a narrowly political project of constitutional government and juridical defense of rights. Rather, it seeks to transform all of human life and the world. Its two revolutions—its anthropological individualism and the voluntarist conception of choice, and its insistence on the human separation from and opposition to nature—created its distinctive and new understanding of liberty as the most extensive possible expansion of the human sphere of autonomous activity.

Liberalism rejects the ancient conception of liberty as the learned capacity of human beings to conquer the slavish pursuit of base and hedonistic desires. This kind of liberty is a condition of self-governance of both city and soul, drawing closely together the individual cultivation and practice of virtue and the shared activities of self-legislation. A central preoccupation of such societies becomes the comprehensive formation and education of individuals and citizens in the art and virtue of self-rule.

Liberalism instead understands liberty as the condition in which one can act freely within the sphere unconstrained by positive law. This concept effectively brings into being what was merely theoretical in its imaginary state of nature, shaping a world in which the theory of natural human individualism becomes ever more a reality, now secured through the architecture of law, politics, economics, and society. Under liberalism, human beings increasingly live in a condition of autonomy in which the threatened anarchy of our purportedly natural condition is controlled and suppressed through the imposition of laws and the corresponding growth of the state. With humanity liberated from constitutive communities (leaving only loose connections) and nature harnessed and controlled, the constructed sphere of autonomous liberty expands seemingly without limit.

Ironically, the more completely the sphere of autonomy is secured, the more comprehensive the state must become. Liberty, so defined, requires liberation from all forms of associations and relationships, from family to church, from schools to village and community, that exerted control over behavior through informal and habituated expectations and norms. These controls were largely cultural, not political—law was less extensive and existed largely as a continuation of cultural norms, the informal expectations of behavior learned through family, church, and community. With the liberation of individuals from these associations, there is more need to regulate behavior through the imposition of positive law. At the same time, as the authority of social norms dissipates, they are increasingly felt to be residual, arbitrary, and oppressive, motivating calls for the state to actively work toward their eradication.

Liberalism thus culminates in two ontological points: the liberated individual and the controlling state. Hobbes's *Levia-*

than perfectly portrayed those realities: the state consists solely of autonomous individuals, and these individuals are "contained" by the state. The individual and the state mark two points of ontological priority.

In this world, gratitude to the past and obligations to the future are replaced by a nearly universal pursuit of immediate gratification: culture, rather than imparting the wisdom and experience of the past so as to cultivate virtues of self-restraint and civility, becomes synonymous with hedonic titillation, visceral crudeness, and distraction, all oriented toward promoting consumption, appetite, and detachment. As a result, superficially self-maximizing, socially destructive behaviors begin to dominate society.

In schools, norms of modesty, comportment, and academic honesty are replaced by widespread lawlessness and cheating (along with increasing surveillance of youth), while in the fraught realm of coming-of-age, courtship norms are replaced by "hookups" and utilitarian sexual encounters. The norm of stable lifelong marriage is replaced by various arrangements that ensure the autonomy of the individuals, whether married or not. Children are increasingly viewed as a limitation upon individual freedom, which contributes to liberalism's commitment to abortion on demand, while overall birth rates decline across the developed world. In the economic realm, the drive for quick profits, often driven by incessant demands for immediate profitability, replaces investment and trusteeship. And in our relationship to the natural world, short-term exploitation of the earth's bounty becomes our birthright, even if it forces our children to deal with shortages of such resources as topsoil and potable water.

Restraint of these activities is understood (if at all) to be the domain of the state's exercise of positive law, not the result of cultivated self-governance born of cultural norms.

Premised on the idea that the basic activity of life is the pursuit of what Hobbes called the "power after power that ceaseth only in death"—which Alexis de Tocqueville later described as "inquietude" or "restlessness"—the endless quest for self-fulfillment and greater power to satisfy human cravings requires ever-accelerating economic growth and pervasive consumption. Liberal society can barely survive the slowing of such growth, and it would collapse if economic growth were to stop or reverse for any length of time. The sole object and justification of this indifference to human ends—of the emphasis on "Right" over "Good"—is the embrace of the liberal human as self-fashioning expressive individual. This aspiration requires that no truly hard choices be made. There are only different lifestyle options.

Liberalism's founders tended to take for granted the persistence of social norms, even as they sought to liberate individuals from the constitutive associations and education in self-limitation that sustained these norms. In its earliest moments, the health and continuity of families, schools, and communities were assumed, while their foundations were being philosophically undermined. This undermining led, in turn, to these goods being undermined in reality, as the norm-shaping power of authoritative institutions grew tenuous with liberalism's advance. In its advanced stage, passive depletion has become active destruction: remnants of associations historically charged with the cultivation of norms are increasingly seen as obstacles to autonomous liberty, and the apparatus of the state is directed toward the task of liberating individuals from such bonds.

In the material and economic realm, liberalism has drawn down on age-old reservoirs of resources in its endeavor to conquer nature. No matter the political program of today's leaders, *more* is the incontestable program. Liberalism can function only by the constant increase of available and consumable material goods, and thus with the constant expansion of nature's conquest and mastery. No person can aspire to a position of political leadership by calling for limits and self-command.

Liberalism was thus a titanic wager that ancient norms of behavior could be lifted in the name of a new form of liberation and that conquering nature would supply the fuel to permit nearly infinite choices. The twin outcomes of this effort—the depletion of moral self-command and the depletion of material resources—make inevitable an inquiry into what comes after liberalism.

If I am right that the liberal project is ultimately self-contradictory and that it culminates in the twin depletions of moral and material reservoirs upon which it has relied, then we face a choice. We can pursue more local forms of self-government by choice, or suffer by default an oscillation between growing anarchy and the increasingly forcible imposition of order by an increasingly desperate state. Taken to its logical conclusion, liberalism's end game is unsustainable in every respect: it cannot perpetually enforce order upon a collection of autonomous individuals increasingly shorn of constitutive social norms, nor can it provide endless material growth in a world of limits. We can either elect a future of self-limitation born of the practice and experience of self-governance in local communities, or we can back inexorably into a future in which extreme license coexists with extreme oppression.

The ancient claim that man is a political animal, and must through the exercise and practice of virtue learned in communities achieve a form of local and communal self-limitation—a condition properly understood as liberty—cannot be denied forever without cost. Currently we attempt to treat the numerous social, economic, and political symptoms of liberalism's liberty, but not the deeper sources of those symptoms, the underlying pathology of liberalism's philosophic commitments. While most commentators regard our current crises—whether understood morally or economically—as a technical problem to be solved by better policy, our most thoughtful citizens must consider whether these crises are the foreshocks of a more systemic quake ahead. Unlike the ancient Romans who, confident in their eternal city, could not imagine a condition after Rome, the rising barbarism within the city forces us now to consider the prospect that a better way awaits.

CHAPTER TWO

Uniting Individualism and Statism

T HE basic division of modern politics since the French Revolution has been between the left and the right, reflecting the respective sides of the French National Assembly, where revolutionaries congregated to the left and royalists gathered to the right. The terms have persisted because they capture two basic and opposite worldviews. The left is characterized by a preference for change and reform, a commitment to liberty and equality, an orientation toward progress and the future, while the right is the party of order and tradition, hierarchy, and a disposition to valorize the past. Whether described as left vs. right, blue vs. red, or liberal vs. conservative, this basic division seems to capture a permanent divide between two fundamental human dispositions, as well as two worldviews that are mutually exclusive and jointly exhaustive of political options. If one of the first questions posed to new parents is whether the baby is a girl or a boy, the question likely to define us from young adulthood is whether we place ourselves on the political left or the political right.

Much contemporary life is organized around this basic division—not only the political machinery, with its plethora of liberal or conservative commentators, media, consultants, pollsters, and politicians sorted according to these labels— but neighborhoods, professions, schools, even one's choice of religion.[1] People are apt to feel more in common with others who share a political outlook even if they are from a different area of the country (or even foreigners), a different ethnic or racial background, and—remarkably, given the history of religious warfare—a different religion. Today, a conservative Protestant evangelical is more likely to befriend and trust an Orthodox Jew or traditionalist Catholic than a liberal Lutheran. A white liberal southerner is likely to be more comfortable revealing political outlooks to a black northern Democrat than to a white conservative in his neighborhood. A progressive homosexual and a liberal Christian will quickly recognize commonalities. More than ever, as we enter an era when the use of sexually differentiating pronouns is discouraged on college campuses and regional differences dissipate into the stew of our national monoculture, political alignment seems to be the one remaining marker that is inescapable and eternal, even natural and inevitable, defining the core of our identity.

Given the extent to which this basic divide shapes the outlooks of nearly every politically aware person living in an advanced liberal society today, it seems almost unthinkable to suggest that it is far less than it seems—and indeed that the apparent unbridgeability of the chasm separating the two sides merely masks a more fundamental, shared worldview. The project of advancing the liberal order takes the superficial form of a battle between seemingly intractable foes, and the energy and acrimony of that contest shrouds a deeper cooperation that ends up advancing liberalism as a whole.

The modern American landscape is occupied by two parties locked in permanent battle. One, deemed "conservative," advances the project of individual liberty and equality of opportunity especially through defense of a free and unfettered market; the other, deemed liberal, aims at securing greater economic and social equality through extensive reliance upon the regulatory and judicial powers of the national government. Our dominant political narrative pits defenders of individual liberty—articulated by such authors of the liberal tradition as John Locke and the American Founding Fathers—against the statism of "progressive" liberals inspired by figures like John Stuart Mill and John Dewey. The two worldviews are regarded as irreconcilable opposites.

These apparently contrary positions are familiar to even the casual observer of contemporary American politics, with conservatives—heirs to classical liberalism—typically decrying statism and liberals—heirs to progressivism—criticizing individualism. The two sides contest every policy over this basic division, touching on contemporary debates over economic and trade policy, health care, welfare, the environment, and a host of hotly contested issues. These battles often come down to a basic debate over whether the ends of the polity are best achieved by market forces with relatively little interference by the state, or by government programs that can distribute benefits and support more justly than the market can achieve.

Thus classical liberals claim that the individual is fundamental and, through an act of contract and consent, brings into existence a limited government. Progressive liberals claim that the individual is never wholly self-sufficient, and that we must instead understand ourselves to be more deeply defined by membership in a larger unit of humanity. Because the two sides appear to be defined not only by a gaping policy divide but by different anthropological assumptions, their deeper shared undercurrent can be difficult to discern.

Individualism and statism advance together, always mutually supportive, and always at the expense of lived and vital relations that stand in contrast to both the starkness of the autonomous individual and the abstraction of our membership in the state. In distinct but related ways, the right and left cooperate in the expansion of both statism and individualism, although from different perspectives, using different means, and claiming different agendas. This deeper cooperation helps to explain how it has happened that contemporary liberal states—whether in Europe or America—have become simultaneously both more statist, with ever more powers and activity vested in central authority, and more individualistic, with people becoming less associated and involved with such mediating institutions as voluntary associations, political parties, churches, communities, and even family. For both "liberals" and "conservatives," the state becomes the main driver of individualism, while individualism becomes the main source of expanding power and authority of the state.

This deeper continuity between right and left derives from two main sources: first, philosophical, with both the classical and progressive liberal traditions arguing ultimately for the central role of the state in the creation and expansion of individualism; and second, practical and political, with this joint philosophical project strengthening an expansion of both state power and individualism. In the previous chapter I briefly limned how the two "sides" of liberalism, while apparently locked in intense contestation, together advance the main objects of the liberal project. In this chapter, I explore this deeper cooperative endeavor in more detail, with particular attention to both the philosophical sources within the liberal tradition and their application in the American context.

Both "classical" and "progressive" liberalism ground the advance of liberalism in individual liberation from the limitations of place, tradition, culture, and any unchosen relationship. Both traditions—for all their differences over means—can be counted as liberal because of this fundamental commitment to liberation of the individual and to the use of natural science, aided by the state, as a primary means for achieving practical liberation from nature's limitations. Thus statism and individualism grow together while local institutions and respect for natural limits diminish. For all their differences, this ambition animated thinkers ranging from John Locke to John Dewey, from Francis Bacon to Francis Bellamy, from Adam Smith to Richard Rorty.

PHILOSOPHICAL SOURCES AND PRACTICAL IMPLICATIONS — CLASSICAL LIBERALISM

This might be a surprising claim, since the philosophy of classical liberalism appears to suggest the opposite: not that the state helps to create the individual, but rather—according to social contract theory—that individuals, free and equal by nature, through consent bring into existence a limited state. Hobbes and Locke both—for all their differences—begin by conceiving natural humans not as parts of wholes but as wholes apart. We are by nature "free and independent," naturally ungoverned and even nonrelational. As Bertrand de Jouvenel quipped about social contractarianism, it was a philosophy conceived by "childless men who must have forgotten their own childhood."[2] Liberty is a condition of complete absence of government and law, in which "all is right"—that is, everything that can be willed by an individual can be done. Even if this condition is shown to be untenable, the definition of natural liberty posited in the "state of nature" becomes a regulative ideal—liberty is ideally the agent's ability to do whatever he likes. In contrast to ancient theory—which understood liberty to be achieved only through virtuous self-government—modern theory defines liberty as the greatest possible pursuit and satisfaction of the appetites, while government is a conventional and unnatural limitation upon this pursuit.

For both Hobbes and Locke, we enter into a social contract not only to secure our survival but to make the exercise of our liberty more secure. Both Hobbes and Locke—but especially Locke—understand that liberty in our prepolitical condition is limited not only by the lawless competition of other individuals but by our recalcitrant and hostile natures. A main goal of Locke's philosophy is to expand the prospects for our liberty—defined as the capacity to satisfy our appetites—through the auspices of the state. Law is not a discipline for self-government but the means for expanding personal freedom: "The end of law is not to abolish or re-strain, but to preserve and enlarge freedom."[3] We accept the terms of the social contract because it will actually increase our personal liberty by eliminating customs and even laws that can be thought to limit individual freedom, even while expanding the prospects for human control over the natural world. Locke writes that the law works to increase liberty, by which he means our liberation from the constraints of the natural world.

Thus, for liberal theory, while the individual "creates" the state through the social contract, in a practical sense, the liberal state "creates" the individual by providing the conditions for the expansion of liberty, increasingly defined as the capacity of humans to expand their mastery over circumstance. Far from there being an inherent conflict between the individual and the state—as so much of modern political reporting would suggest—liberalism establishes a deep and profound connection: its ideal of liberty can be realized only through a powerful state. If the expansion of freedom is secured by law, then the opposite also holds true in practice: increasing freedom requires the expansion of law. The state does not merely serve as a referee between contesting individuals; in securing our capacity to engage in productive activities, especially commerce, it establishes a condition in reality that existed in theory only in the state of nature: the ever-increasing achievement of the autonomous individual.

Thus one of the liberal state's main roles becomes the active liberation of individuals from any limiting conditions. At the forefront of liberal theory is the liberation from natural limitations on the achievement of our desires—one of the central aims of life, according to Locke, being the "indolency of the body." A main agent of that liberation becomes commerce, the expansion of opportunities and materials by which not only to realize existing desires but even to create new ones we did not know we had. The state becomes charged with extending the sphere of commerce, particularly with enlarging the range of trade, production, and mobility.[4] The expansion of markets and the infrastructure necessary for that expansion do not result from "spontaneous order"; rather, they require an extensive and growing state structure, which at times must extract submission from the system's recalcitrant or unwilling participants. Initially, this effort is exerted on local domestic economy, in which the state must enforce rationalization and imposition of depersonalized modern markets. Eventually, however, this project becomes a main driver of liberal imperialism, an imperative justified among others by John Stuart Mill in his treatise *Considerations on Representative Government*, where he calls for compulsion over "uncivilized" peoples in order that they might lead productive economic lives, even if they must be "for a while compelled to it," including through the institution of "personal slavery."[5]

One of the main goals of the expansion of commerce is the liberation of embedded individuals from their traditional ties and relationships. The liberal state serves not only the reactive function of umpire and protector of individual liberty; it also takes on an active role of "liberating" individuals who, in the view of the state, are prevented from making wholly free choices as liberal agents. At the heart of liberal theory is the supposition that the individual is the basic unit of human existence, the only natural human entity that exists.

Liberal practice then seeks to expand the conditions for this individual's realization. The individual is to be liberated from all the partial and limiting affiliations that preceded the liberal state, if not by force then by constantly lowering the barriers to exit. The state claims to govern all groupings within the society: it is the final arbiter of legitimate and illegitimate groupings, and from its point of view, streamlining the relationship between the individual and the liberal state.

In a reversal of the scientific method, what is advanced as a philosophical set of arguments is then instantiated in reality. The individual as a disembedded, self-interested economic actor didn't exist in any actual state of nature but rather was the creation of an elaborate intervention by the incipient state in early modernity, at the beginnings of the liberal order. The imposition of the liberal order is accompanied by the legitimizing myth that its form was freely chosen by unencumbered individuals; that it was the consequence of extensive state intervention is ignored by all but a few scholars. Few works have made this intervention clearer than the historian and sociologist Karl Polanyi's classic study *The Great Transformation*.[6] Polanyi describes how economic arrangements were separated from particular cultural and religious contexts in which those arrangements were understood to serve moral ends—and posits that these contexts limited not only actions but even prevented the understanding that economic actions could be properly undertaken to advance individual interests and priorities. Economic exchange so ordered, Polanyi argues, placed a priority on the main ends of social, political, and religious life—the sustenance of community order and flourishing of families within that order.[7] The understanding of an economy based upon the accumulated calculations of self-maximizing individuals was not, properly speaking, a market. A market-*place* was understood to be an actual physical space within the social order, not an autonomous, theoretical space for exchanges conducted by abstracted utility maximizers.

According to Polanyi, the replacement of this economy required a deliberate and often violent reshaping of local economies, most often by elite economic and state actors disrupting and displacing traditional communities and practices. The "individuation" of people required not only the separation of markets from social and religious contexts but people's acceptance that their labor and its products were nothing more than commodities subject to price mechanisms, a transformative way of considering people and nature alike in newly utilitarian and individualistic terms. Yet market liberalism required treating both people and natural resources as these "fictitious commodities"—as material for use in industrial processes—in order to disassociate markets from morals and "re-train" people to think of themselves as individuals separate from nature and one another. As Polanyi pithily says of this transformation, "laissez-faire was planned."[8]

This process was repeated countless times in the history of modern political economy: in efforts to eradicate the medieval guilds, in the enclosure controversy, in state suppression of "Luddites," in state support for owners over organized labor, and in government efforts to empty the nation's farmlands via mechanized, industrial farming. It was, in complex ways, an underlying motive during the American Civil War, which, for all its legitimacy in eliminating slavery, also decisively brought the state-backed expansion of a national economic system, opposition to which was forever stained by guilt by association with southern slavery.[9] We see its legacy today in the ongoing expansion of global markets through free-trade agreements ardently supported by so-called conservatives, often with the aim of disrupting and ultimately displacing native cultures that might be of concern both to Burkean conservatives and to Marxist-leaning critics of relentless globalization.[10] The state's role in enforcing the existence of a national market has been reinforced in recent years by efforts to roll back various state-based environmental standards— ironically, an activity most ardently embraced by "conservative" Republicans who are otherwise strident defenders of "states' rights."[11]

From the dawn of modernity to contemporary headlines, the proponents and heirs of classical liberalism—those whom we today call "conservative"—have at best offered lip service to the defense of "traditional values" while its leadership class unanimously supports the main instrument of practical individualism in our modern world, the global "free market." This market—like all markets—while justified in the name of "laissez-faire," in fact depends on constant state energy, intervention, and support, and has consistently been supported by classical liberals for its solvent effect on traditional relationships, cultural norms, generational thinking, and the practices and habits that subordinate market considerations to concerns born of interpersonal bonds and charity. Claiming that the radical individual imagined by liberal theory was a "given," liberal practice advanced this normative ideal through an ever-burgeoning state that ceaselessly expanded not in spite of individualism, but to bring about its realization.

One of the consequences of the political, social, and economic dynamism unleashed by classical liberalism was the widespread sense that it had underestimated the capacity for human transformation as well. Dewey, for example, in his short book *Individualism, Old and New*, praises the "old" liberalism for its success in "liquefying static property" of the type that was prevalent in feudal times, and for eliminating the local bases of social life as the economic and political system became visibly more national and "interdependent." He dismisses the "romantic" individualism that had animated the American belief in self-reliance (here echoing Frederick Jackson Turner's observations that the age of the American frontier had come to a close), instead calling for recognition that it was empirically true that Americans were now part of a "social whole" from which no individual could be understood to exist in separation.[12]

The "old individualism" had successfully undermined any vestiges of aristocratic society or Jeffersonian agrarianism, but the nation had not yet made the leap into a new "organic" reconciliation of individual and society. The "liberalism of the past" had created the conditions that now required its own supercession: a new liberalism was now in view, needing a push by philosophically and socially sensitive thinkers like Dewey to realize humanity's self-transformative potential.

Herbert Croly similarly saw a transformation taking place, particularly in the national system of commerce, culture, and identity. But this national system was still animated by a belief in Jeffersonian independence even as in fact it reflected new forms of interdependence. He called for the creation of a "New Republic" (the name of the journal he cofounded) that would achieve "Jeffersonian ends by Hamiltonian means." Democracy could no longer mean individual self-reliance based upon the freedom of individuals to act in accordance with their own wishes. Instead, it must be infused with a social and even religious set of commitments that would lead people to recognize their participation in the "brotherhood of mankind." This aspiration had been thwarted heretofore by antiquated belief in individual self-determination, neglectful of a profound and growing interdependence that was now generating the potential for "the gradual creation of a higher type of individual and higher life."[13] Walter Rauschenbusch was to echo this sentiment in his call to establish the "Kingdom of God" on earth, a new and more deeply social form of democracy that "would not accept human nature as it is, but move it in the direction of its improvement." Rauschenbusch, by overcoming the individualistic self-interest that he saw informing even traditional Christian theology—whose object had traditionally been individual salvation—envisioned, like Dewey and Croly, the "consummation" of democracy as the "perfection of human nature."[14]

While one may see collectivist economic arrangements in these thinkers' practical recommendations—Dewey, for instance, calls for "public socialism," and Croly writes in support of "flagrant socialism"—it would be mistaken to conclude that they do not endorse the inviolability and dignity of the individual. A consistent theme in both men's work is that only by eliminating the cramped and limiting individualism of "old liberalism" can a truer and better form of "individuality" emerge. Only complete liberation from the shackles of unfreedom—including especially the manacles of economic degradation and inequality—can bring the emergence of a new and better individuality. The apotheosis of democracy, they argue, will lead to a reconciliation of the "Many" and the "One," a reconciliation of our social nature and our individuality. John Dewey writes, for instance, that "a stable recovery of *individuality* waits upon an elimination of the older economic and political *individualism*, an elimination that will liberate imagination and endeavor for the task of making corporate society contribute to the free culture of its members."

While we will have to wait for the complete elimination of old liberalism to know fully how that reconciliation of "individuality" and "corporate society" will be achieved, what is clear from these central and formative arguments of the progressive liberal tradition is that only by overcoming classical liberalism can true liberalism emerge. The argument still continues over whether this represents a fundamental break with, or fundamental fruition of, the liberal project.

The most apt recent symbol of the progressive state's role in "creating" the individual was a fictional woman who famously formed part of President Obama's campaign for reelection in 2012—a woman who, like Cher or Madonna, needed only a single name, Julia. Julia appeared briefly toward the beginning of Obama's campaign as a series of internet slides in which it was demonstrated that she had achieved her dreams through a series of government programs that, throughout her life, had enabled various milestones. Part of the effort to show the existence of a Republican "war on women," the ad campaign "Life of Julia" was designed to convince female voters that only progressive liberals would support the government programs that would help them achieve a better life.[15]

While the "Life of Julia" campaign seemed thus designed for liberals who generally supported government programs that helped foster economic opportunity and greater equality, Julia was nevertheless someone who could not be an object of admiration without the background appeal of conservative liberalism's valorization of the autonomous individual as the normative ideal of human liberty. If the positive portrayal of Julia's extensive reliance upon government aid tended to make the right blind to the ad's fundamentally liberal ideal of autonomy, the left was barely cognizant that the aim of this assistance was to create the most perfectly autonomous individual since Hobbes and Locke dreamed up the State of Nature. In Julia's world there are only Julia and the government, with the very brief exception of a young child who appears in one slide—with no evident father—and is quickly whisked away by a government-sponsored yellow bus, never to be seen again. Otherwise, Julia has achieved a life of perfect autonomy, courtesy of a massive, sometimes intrusive, always solicitous, ever-present government. The world portrayed by "Life of Julia" is an updated version of the frontispiece of Hobbes's *Leviathan*, in which there only exist individuals and the sovereign state—the former creating and giving legitimacy to the latter, the latter ensuring a safe and secure life for the individuals who brought it into being. The main difference is that while Hobbes's story is meant as a thought experiment, "The Life of Julia" is meant to depict present-day reality. But the ad makes increasingly clear that its story is the very opposite of Hobbes's: it is the liberal state that creates the individual. Through the increasingly massive and all-encompassing Leviathan, we are finally free of one another.

Thus the two sides of the liberal project wage a ceaseless and absorbing contest over means, the ideal avenue for liberating the individual from constitutive relationships, from unchosen traditions, from restraining custom. Behind the lines, however, both have consistently sought the expansion of the sphere of liberation in which the individual can best pursue his or her preferred lifestyle, leading to mutual support of the expansion of the state as the requisite setting in which the autonomous individual could come into being. While "conservative" liberals express undying hostility to state expansion, they consistently turn to its capacity to secure national and international markets as a way of overcoming any local forms of governance or traditional norms that might limit the market's role in the life of a community.[16] And while "progressive" liberals declaim the expansive state as the ultimate protector of individual liberty, they insist that it must be limited when it comes to enforcement of "manners and morals," preferring the open marketplace of individual "buyers and sellers," especially in matters of sexual practice and infinitely fluid sexual identity, the definition of family, and individual choices over ending one's own life. The modern liberal state consistently expands to enlarge our self-definition as "consumers"—a word more often used today to describe denizens of the liberal nation-state than "citizens"—while entertaining us with a cataclysmic battle between two sides that many begin to rightly suspect aren't that different after all.

At the heart of liberal theory and practice is the preeminent role of the state as agent of individualism. This very liberation in turn generates liberalism's self-reinforcing circle, wherein the increasingly disembedded individual ends up strengthening the state that is its own author. From the perspective of liberalism, it is a virtuous circle, but from the standpoint of human flourishing, it is one of the deepest sources of liberal pathology.

An earlier generation of philosophers and sociologists noted the psychological condition that led increasingly dislocated and disassociated selves to derive their basic identity from the state. These analyses—in landmark works such as Hannah Arendt's *The Origins of Totalitarianism*, Erich Fromm's *Escape from Freedom*, and Robert Nisbet's *The Quest for Community*—recognized, from various perspectives and disciplines, that a signal feature of modern totalitarianism was that it arose and came to power through the discontents of people's isolation and loneliness. A population seeking to fill the void left by the weakening of more local memberships and associations was susceptible to a fanatical willingness to identify completely with a distant and abstract state. While this analysis attracted adherents in years following the fall of Nazism and the rise of communism, it has since declined, suggesting that many contemporary thinkers do not think it applies to liberal ideology.[17] Yet there is no reason to suppose the basic political psychology works any differently today.

Nisbet remains an instructive guide. In *The Quest for Community*, his 1953 analysis of the rise of modern ideologies,

Nisbet argued that the active dissolution of traditional human communities and institutions had given rise to a condition in which a basic human need—"the quest for community"—was no longer being met. Statism arose as a violent reaction against this feeling of atomization. As naturally political and social creatures, people require a thick set of constitutive bonds in order to function as fully formed human beings. Shorn of the deepest ties to family (nuclear as well as extended), place, community, region, religion, and culture, and deeply shaped to believe that these forms of association are limits upon their autonomy, deracinated humans seek belonging and self-definition through the only legitimate form of organization remaining available to them: the state. Nisbet saw the rise of fascism and communism as the predictable consequence of the liberal attack upon smaller associations and communities. Those ideologies offered a new form of belonging by adopting the evocations and imagery of the associations they had displaced, above all by offering a new form of quasi-religious membership, a kind of church of the state. Our "community" was now to consist of countless fellow humans who shared an abstract allegiance to a political entity that would assuage all of our loneliness, alienation, and isolation. It would provide for our wants and needs; all it asked in return was complete devotion to the state and the elimination of any allegiance to any other intermediary entity. To provide for a mass public, more power to the central authority was asked and granted. Thus Nisbet concludes, "It is impossible to understand the massive concentrations of political power in the twentieth century, appearing so paradoxically, or it has seemed, right after a century and a half of individualism in economics and morals, unless we see the close relationship that prevailed all through the nineteenth century between individualism and State power and between both of these together and the general weakening of the area of association that lies intermediate to man and the State."[18]

Beyond psychological longing, the ascent of the state as object of allegiance was a necessary consequence of liberalism's practical effects. Having shorn people's ties to the vast web of intermediating institutions that sustained them, the expansion of individualism deprived them of recourse to those traditional places of support and sustenance. The more individuated the polity, the more likely that a mass of individuals would inevitably turn to the state in times of need. This observation, echoing one originally made by Tocqueville, suggests that individualism is not the alternative to statism but its very cause. Tocqueville, unlike so many of his current conservative and progressive readers, understood that individualism was not the solution to the problem of an increasingly encompassing centralized state but the source of its increasing power. As he wrote in *Democracy in America,*

> So . . . no man is obliged to put his powers at the disposal of another, and no one has any claim of right to substantial support from his fellow man, each is both independent and weak. These two conditions, which must be neither seen quite separately nor confused, give the citizen of a democracy extremely contradictory instincts. He is full of confidence and pride in his independence among his equals, but from time to time his weakness makes him feel the need for some outside help which he cannot expect from any of his fellows, for they are both impotent and cold. In this extremity he naturally turns his eyes toward that huge entity [the tutelary state] which alone stands out above the universal level of abasement. His needs, and

even more his longings, continually put him in mind of that
entity, and he ends by regarding it as the sole and necessary
support of his individual weakness.[19]

The individualism arising from the philosophy and practice of liberalism, far from fundamentally opposing an increasingly centralized state, both required it and in fact increased its power. Indeed, individualism and statism have
powerfully combined to all but rout the vestiges of pre- and
often nonliberal communities animated by a philosophy and
practice distinct from statist individualism. Today's classical
liberals and progressive liberals remain locked in a battle for
their preferred end game—whether we will be a society of
ever more perfectly liberated, autonomous individuals or ever
more egalitarian members of the global "community"—but
while this debate continues apace, the two sides agree on their
end while absorbing our attention in disputes over the means,
thus combining in a pincer movement to destroy the vestiges
of the classical practices and virtues that they both despise.

The expansion of liberalism rests upon a vicious and
reinforcing cycle in which state expansion secures the end of
individual fragmentation, in turn requiring further state expansion to control a society without shared norms, practices,
or beliefs. Liberalism thus increasingly requires a legal and
administrative regime, driven by the imperative of replacing
all nonliberal forms of support for human flourishing (such as
schools, medicine, and charity), and hollowing any deeply
held sense of shared future or fate among the citizenry. Informal relationships are replaced by administrative directives,
political policies, and legal mandates, undermining voluntary
civic membership and requiring an ever-expanding state

apparatus to ensure social cooperation. The threat and evidence of declining civic norms require centralized surveillance, highly visible police presence, and a carceral state to control the effects of its own successes while diminishing civic trust and mutual commitment.

The ways in which the individualist philosophy of classical liberalism and the statist philosophy of progressive liberalism end up reinforcing each other often go undetected. Although conservative liberals claim to defend not only a free market but family values and federalism, the only part of the conservative agenda that has been continuously and successfully implemented during their recent political ascendance is economic liberalism, including deregulation, globalization, and the protection of titanic economic inequalities. And while progressive liberals claim to advance a shared sense of national destiny and solidarity that should decrease the advance of an individualist economy and reduce income inequality, the only part of the left's political agenda that has triumphed has been the project of personal and especially sexual autonomy. Is it mere coincidence that both parties, despite their claims to be locked in a political death grip, mutually advance the cause of liberal autonomy and inequality?

CHAPTER THREE

Liberalism as Anticulture

THE dual expansion of the state and personal autonomy rests extensively on the weakening and eventual loss of particular cultures, and their replacement not by a single liberal culture but by a pervasive and encompassing *anticulture*. What is popularly called a "culture," often modified by an adjective—for instance, "pop culture" or "media culture" or "multiculturalism"—is in fact a sign of the evisceration of culture as a set of generational customs, practices, and rituals that are grounded in local and particular settings. As Mario Vargas Llosa has written, "The idea of culture has broadened to such an extent that, although nobody has dared to say this explicitly, it has disappeared. It has become an ungraspable, multitudinous and figurative ghost."[1] The only forms of shared cultural "liturgy" that remain are celebrations of the liberal state and the liberal market. National holidays have become occasions for shopping, and shopping holy days such as "Black Friday" have become national holidays. These forms of abstract membership mark a populace delinked from particular affiliations and devotions, which are transferred to—in a video played at the 2012 Democratic National Convention—"the only thing we all belong to," the liberal state. This ambitious claim failed to note that the only thing we *all* belong to is the global market, an encompassing entity that contains all political organizations and their citizenry, now redefined as consumers. The liturgies of nation and market are woven closely together (the apogee of which is the celebration of commercials during the Super Bowl), simultaneously nationalist and consumerist celebrations of abstracted membership that reify individuated selves held together by depersonalized commitments. In the politically nationalist and economically globalist setting, these contentless liturgies often take the form of two minutes of obligatory patriotism in which a member of the armed services appears during pauses in a sporting event for reverential applause before everyone gets back to the serious business of distracted consumption. The show of superficial thanks for a military with which few have any direct connection leaves an afterglow that distracts from the harder question of whether the national military ultimately functions to secure the global market and so support the construction of abstracted, deracinated, and consumptive selves.

THE THREE PILLARS OF LIBERAL ANTICULTURE

Liberal anticulture rests on three pillars: first, the wholesale conquest of nature, which consequently makes nature into an independent object requiring salvation by the notional elimination of humanity; second, a new experience of time as a pastless present in which the future is a foreign land; and third, an order that renders place fungible and bereft of definitional meaning. These three cornerstones of human experience—nature, time and place—form the basis of culture, and liberalism's success is premised upon their uprooting and replacement with facsimiles that bear the same names.

The advance of this anticulture takes two primary forms. Anticulture is the consequence of a regime of standardizing law replacing widely observed informal norms that come to be discarded as forms of oppression; and it is the simultaneous consequence of a universal and homogenous market, resulting in a monoculture that, like its agricultural analogue, colonizes and destroys actual cultures rooted in experience, history, and place. These two visages of the liberal anticulture thus free us from other specific people and embedded relationships, replacing custom with abstract and depersonalized law, liberating us from personal obligations and debts, replacing what have come to be perceived as burdens on our individual autonomous freedom with pervasive legal threat and generalized financial indebtedness. In the effort to secure the radical autonomy of individuals, liberal law and the liberal market replace actual culture with an encompassing anticulture.

This anticulture is the arena of our liberty—yet increasingly, it is rightly perceived as the locus of our bondage and even a threat to our continued existence. The simultaneous heady joy and gnawing anxieties of a liberated humanity, shorn of the compass of tradition and inheritance that were the hallmarks of embedded culture, are indicators of liberalism's waxing success and accumulating failure. The paradox is our growing belief that we are thralls to the very sources of our liberation—pervasive legal surveillance and control of people alongside technological control of nature. As the empire of liberty grows, the reality of liberty recedes. The anticulture of liberalism—supposedly the source of our liberation—accelerates liberalism's success and demise.

Anticulture and the Conquest of Nature

One of liberalism's main revolutions was not in the narrowly political realm but in its disassociation of nature from culture. The fundamental premise of liberalism is that the natural condition of man is defined above all by the absence of culture, and that, by contrast, the presence of culture marks existence of artifice and convention, the simultaneous effort to alter but conform to nature. In its earliest articulation, liberal anthropology assumed that "natural man" was a cultureless creature, existing in a "state of nature" noteworthy for the absence of any artifice created by humans. For the protoliberal Hobbes, the state of nature was explicitly the sphere where no culture was possible, because it lacked the conditions in which stability, continuity, cultural transmission, and memory could exist. Jean-Jacques Rousseau, for all his opposition to Hobbes, conceived the state of nature as a place of relative peace and stability, but nevertheless strikingly similar to Hobbes's in its absence of cultural forms, and fundamentally identical in the radical autonomy of its protohuman inhabitants. Despite its romantic rejection of the cold, rationalist, and utilitarian Hobbesian picture of humanity, Rousseau's primitivist alternative nevertheless reveals continuity among all iterations of liberalism in its fundamental commitment to the severance of nature from culture.

While today we can still speak of differences of "nature" and "nurture," even the possibility of a divide between these two would have been incomprehensible to preliberal humanity. The revolutionary nature of the break introduced by liberalism is discernible even in the very word "culture." "Culture" is a word with deep connections to natural forms and processes, most obviously in words such as "agriculture" or "cultivate." Just as the potential of a plant or animal isn't possible without cultivation, so it was readily understood that the human creature's best potential simply could not be realized without good culture. This was so evident to ancient thinkers that the first several chapters of Plato's *Republic* are devoted not to a discussion of political forms but to the kinds of stories that are appropriate for children. In a suggestive statement winding up his introductory chapter in *The Politics*, Aristotle declares that the first lawmaker is especially praiseworthy for inaugurating governance over "food and sex," that is, the two elemental human desires that are most in need of cultivation and civilization: for food, the development of manners that encourage a moderate appetite and civilized consumption, and for sex, the cultivation of customs and habits of courtship, mannered interaction between the sexes, and finally marriage as the "container" of the otherwise combustible and fraught domain of sexuality. People who are "uncultivated" in the consumption of both food and sex, Aristotle observed, are the most vicious of creatures, literally consuming other humans to slake their base and untutored appetites. Far from being understood as opposites of human nature, customs and manners were understood to be derived from, governed by, and necessary to the realization of human nature.

A core ambition of liberalism is the liberation of such appetites from the artificial constraints of culture—either to liberate them entirely as a condition of our freedom, or, where they require constraint, to place them under the uniform and homogenized governance of promulgated law rather than the inconstant impositions and vagaries of diverse cultures. While liberalism describes itself as mainly an effort to constrain and limit government, its earliest architects readily admitted that a powerful and often arbitrary government—acting upon "prerogative"—was necessary to secure the basic conditions of freedom and its requisite stability. From the outset, proponents of liberalism understood that cultural constraints over expression and pursuit of appetite were obstacles to the realization of a society premised upon unleashing erstwhile vices (such as greed) as engines of economic dynamism, and that state power might be required to overturn cultural institutions responsible for containing such appetites.[2] Today, with the success of the liberal project in the economic sphere, the powers of the liberal state are increasingly focused on dislocating those remaining cultural institutions that were responsible for governance of consumer and sexual appetite—purportedly in the name of freedom and equality, but above all in a comprehensive effort to displace cultural forms as the ground condition of liberal liberty. Only constraints approved by the liberal state itself can finally be acceptable. The assumption is that legitimate limits upon liberty can arise only from the authority of the consent-based liberal state.

The liberation of the autonomous individual requires not only the waxing state apparatus but the expansive project of conquering nature. This end as well rested most fundamentally upon the notional, and then increasingly real, elimination of culture. Culture is the "convention" by which humans interact responsibly with nature, at once conforming to its governance while introducing human ingenuity and invention within its limits and boundaries.

A healthy culture is akin to healthy agriculture—while clearly a form of human artifice, agriculture that takes into account local conditions (place) intends to maintain fecundity over generations (time), and so must work with the facts of given nature, not approach nature as an obstacle to the attainment of one's unbound appetites. Modern, industrialized agriculture works on the liberal model that apparent natural limits are to be overcome through short-term solutions whose consequences will be left for future generations. These solutions include the introduction of petroleum-based fertilizers that increase crop yields but contribute to hypoxic zones in lakes and oceans; genetically engineered crops that encourage increased use of herbicides and pesticides and whose genetic lines can't be contained or predicted; the widespread use of plant monocultures that displace local varieties and local practices; and the use in cattle of antibiotics that have accelerated genetic mutations in bacteria and thus decreased these medicines' usefulness for the human population. Industrial processes like these ignore the distinctive demands of local culture and practices and rely fundamentally on the elimination of existing farming cultures as the essence of agriculture. While purportedly forward-looking, this approach is profoundly presentist and placeless.

A culture develops above all in awareness of nature's limits, offerings, and demands. This awareness is not "theorized" but is a lived reality that often cannot be described until it has ceased to exist.[3] Liberalism, by contrast, has aimed consistently at disassociating cultural forms from nature. The effect is at once to liberate humans from acknowledgement of nature's limits while rendering culture into wholly relativist belief and practice, untethered from anything universal or enduring. The aim of mastering nature toward the end of liberating humanity from its limits—a project inaugurated in the thought of Francis Bacon—was simultaneously an assault on cultural norms and practices developed alongside nature.

The imperative to overcome culture as part of the project of mastering nature was expressed with forthright clarity by John Dewey, one of liberalism's great heroes. Dewey insisted that the progress of liberation rested especially upon the active control of nature, and hence required the displacement of traditional beliefs and culture that reflected a backward and limiting regard for the past. He described these two approaches to the human relationship to nature as "civilized" versus "savage." The savage tribe manages to live in the desert, he wrote, by adapting itself to the natural limits of its environment; thus "its adaptation involves a maximum of accepting, tolerating, putting up with things as they are, a maximum of passive acquiescence, and a minimum of active control, of subjection to use." A "civilized people" in the same desert also adapts; but "it introduces irrigation; it searches the world for plants and animals that will flourish under such conditions; it improves, by careful selection, those which are growing there. As a consequence, the wilderness blossoms as a rose. The savage is merely habituated; the civilized man has habits which transform the environment."[4]

Dewey traced his thought back to Francis Bacon, whom he considered the most important thinker in history. Bacon, he wrote in his *Reconstruction in Philosophy*, teaches that "scientific laws do not lie on the surface of nature. They are hidden, and must be wrested from nature by an active and elaborate technique of inquiry." The scientist "must force the apparent facts of nature into forms different to those in which they familiarly present themselves; and thus make them tell the truth about themselves, as torture may compel an unwilling witness to reveal what he has been concealing."[5] Today's liberals recoil from such bald expressions of hubris, but rather than reject Dewey's effort to eliminate culture toward the end of dominating nature, they are inclined to accept the liberal belief in human separateness from nature and insist upon the conquest of humanity—whether through the technological control of the natural world ("conservative" liberals) or the technological control of reproduction and mastery of the human genetic code ("progressive" liberals). A core feature of the liberal project is antipathy to culture as a deep relationship with a nature that defines and limits human nature.

Liberal Timelessness

More than a system of government or legal and political order, liberalism is about redefining the human perception of time. It is an effort to transform the experience of time, in particular the relationship of past, present, and future.

Social contract theory was about the abstraction of the individual not only from human relations and places but also from time. It depicts a history-less and timeless condition, a thought experiment intended to be applicable at any and all times. The most obvious reason for this conceit—that we be invited to see its relevance in any circumstance, as Hobbes famously argues in pointing out such everyday activities as locking our chests and doors—obscures the deeper lesson that humans are by nature creatures who live in an eternal present. The conceit appeals not to some historical "social contract" that we must look back to for guidance but to the continual, ongoing belief that we are always by nature autonomous choosing agents who perceive advantage for ourselves in an ongoing contractual arrangement. Once again, however, liberal theory posits a form of existence that contradicts what most people's actual experience was before liberal society brought its "natural" conditions into existence. Only with the ascendancy of liberal political orders does the experience of history in its fullest temporal dimension wane, and a pervasive presentism become a dominant feature of life. This condition is achieved especially through the dismantling of culture, the vessel of the human experience of time.

The development of progressivism within liberalism is only a further iteration of this pervasive presentism, a kind of weaponized timelessness. Like classical liberalism, progressivism is grounded in a deep hostility toward the past, particularly tradition and custom. While widely understood to be future-oriented, it in fact rests on simultaneous assumptions that contemporary solutions must be liberated from past answers but that the future will have as much regard for our present as we have for the past. The future is an unknown country, and those who live in a present arrayed in hostility to the past must acquire indifference toward, and a simple faith in, a better if unknowable future. Those whose view of time is guided by such belief implicitly understand that their "achievements" are destined for the dustbin of history, given that the future will regard us as backward and necessarily superseded. Every generation must live for itself. Liberalism makes humanity into mayflies, and unsurprisingly, its culmination has led each generation to accumulate scandalous levels of debt to be left for its children, while rapacious exploitation of resources continues in the progressive belief that future generations will devise a way to deal with the depletions.

This transformation of the experience of time has been described in terms of two distinct forms of time: whereas preliberal humanity experienced time as cyclical, modernity thinks of it as linear. While suggestive and enlightening, this linear conception of time is still premised on a fundamental continuity between past, present, and future. Liberalism in its several guises in fact advances a conception of fractured time, of time fundamentally disconnected, and shapes humans to experience different times as if they were radically different countries.

Alexis de Tocqueville noted the connection between the rise of liberal orders and the experience of fractured time. He observed that liberal democracy would be marked above all by a tendency toward presentism. In its egalitarianism and especially in its rejection of aristocracy, it would be suspicious of the past and future, encouraging instead a kind of stunted individualism. Aristocracy, Tocqueville wrote, "links everybody, from peasant to king, in one long chain. Democracy breaks the chain and frees each link. . . . Thus, not only does democracy make men forget their ancestors, but also clouds their view of their descendants and isolates them from their contemporaries. Each man is forever thrown back upon himself alone and there is a danger that he may be shut up in the solitude of his own heart."[6]

Tocqueville perceived the way in which "fractured time" generates individualism, which in turn would have profound social, political, and economic consequences as the underlying logic of liberal democracy advances. He fretted especially about the inability of a liberal democratic people to see their own lives and actions as part of a continuum of time, and hence to consider long-term implications of their actions and deeds as part of a long-term human community. While a constitutive feature of an aristocratic age was the pervasive understanding of oneself as defined by one's place in a generational order, a hallmark of democracy was to "break" that chain in the name and pursuit of liberation of the individual. While beneficial for individual liberation from generational definition and debts, the fractured experience of time was to have baleful political implications. Modern liberal democracies, Tocqueville believed, would have a powerful tendency to act only for the short term, thus to discount the consequences of their actions upon future generations:

> Once [liberal democrats] have grown accustomed not to think about what will happen after their life, they easily fall back into a complete and brutish indifference about the future, an attitude all too well suited to certain propensities in human nature. As soon as they have lost the way of relying chiefly upon distant hopes, they are naturally led to want to satisfy their least desires at once. . . . [Thus] there is always a danger that men will give way to ephemeral and casual desires and that, wholly

renouncing whatever cannot be acquired without protracted effort, they may never achieve anything great or calm or lasting.[7]

Tocqueville notes that the propensity to think only within the context of one's own lifespan, and to focus on satisfaction of immediate and baser pleasures, is a basic "propensity in human nature." To chasten, educate, and moderate this basic instinct is the fruit of broader political, social, religious, and familial structures, practices, and expectations. Liberalism stresses our liberation from continuous time as a basic feature of our nature, and thus regards such formative institutions, structures, and practices as obstacles to the achievement of our untrammeled individuality. The disassembling of those cultural forms that tutor our presentism and instruct us that a distinctive feature of our humanity is our capacity to remember and to promise renders us at once free, and trapped by "brutish indifference" to any time outside our eternal present.

Tocqueville perceived that this same "brutish indifference" would manifest itself not only politically but economically as well. Dissolving the practices, along with the structures, that draw people out of temporal narrowness, he feared, would have the effect of separating people's capacity to discern a shared fate. Fractured time, and the resultant escape into the "solitude of our own hearts," would lead to self-congratulation and actual physical as well as psychic separation of those who were economically successful from those less fortunate. In effect, he predicted that a new aristocracy would arise, but that its "brutish indifference" born of temporal fracturing would lead it to be worse than the aristocracy it was replacing. "The territorial aristocracy of past ages was obliged by law, or thought itself obliged by custom, to come to the help of its servants and to relieve their distress. But the industrial aristocracy of our day, when it has impoverished and brutalized the men it uses, abandons them in their time of crisis to public charity to feed them. . . . Between workman and master there are frequent relations, but no true association."[8] The fracturing of time is embraced as a form of freedom, a liberation especially of personal obligations we have to those with whom we share a past, a future, and even—ultimately—the present itself.

A better way to understand culture is as a kind of collective trust. Culture is the practice of full temporality, an institution that connects the present to the past and the future. As the Greeks understood, the mother of culture—of the Nine Muses—was Mnemosyne, whose name means "memory." Culture educates us about our generational debts and obligations. At its best, it is a tangible inheritance of the past, one that each of us is obligated to regard with the responsibilities of trusteeship. It is itself an education in the full dimension of human temporality, meant to abridge our temptation to live within the present, with the attendant dispositions of ingratitude and irresponsibility that such a narrowing of temporality encourages. Preserved in discrete human inheritances—arts, literature, music, architecture, history, law, religion—culture expands the human experience of time, making both the past and the future present to creatures who otherwise experience only the present moment.

Liberalism as Nowhere and Everywhere

Liberalism valorizes placelessness. Its "state of nature" posits a view from nowhere: abstract individuals in equally abstract places. Not only does liberalism rest on the anthropological assumption that humans are from no one—emerging, as Hobbes described, "from the earth like mushrooms and grown up without any obligation to each other"—but that we are from nowhere.⁹ The place where one happens to be born and raised is as arbitrary as one's parents, one's religion, or one's customs. One should consider oneself primarily a free chooser, of place as of all relationships, institutions, and beliefs.

This is not to say that humans who are more firmly embedded within cultural settings don't sometimes set out for new pastures. But liberalism sets a distinctive and radically placeless "default" that begins as theory but eventually reshapes the world in its image. As Thomas Jefferson articulated in the Lockean tuneup that preceded his drafting of the Declaration of Independence, the most fundamental right defining the liberal human is the right to leave the place of one's birth.¹⁰ Our default condition is homelessness.

This placeless default is one of the preeminent ways that liberalism subtly, unobtrusively, and pervasively undermines all cultures and liberates individuals into the irresponsibility of anticulture. No thinker has more ably discerned the deracinating effects of modern life than the Kentucky farmer, novelist, poet, and essayist Wendell Berry. An unapologetic defender of community in place, Berry regards community as a rich and varied set of personal relationships, a complex of practices and traditions drawn from a store of common memory and tradition, and a set of bonds forged between a people and a place that—because of this situatedness—is not portable, mobile, fungible, or transferable.¹¹ Community is more than a collection of self-interested individuals brought together to seek personal advancement. Rather, it "lives and acts by the common virtues of trust, goodwill, forbearance, self-restraint, compassion, and forgiveness."[12]

Berry is not hesitant to acknowledge that community is a place of constraint and limits. Indeed, in this simple fact lies its great attraction. Properly conceived, community is the appropriate setting for flourishing human life—flourishing that requires culture, discipline, constraint, and forms. At the most elemental level (in an echo of Aristotle, if an unconscious one), community is both derived from and in turn makes possible healthful family life. Absent the supports of communal life, family life is hard-pressed to flourish. This is because family life is premised, in Berry's view, on the discipline of otherwise individualistic tendencies toward narrow self-fulfillment, particularly erotic ones. He commends

> arrangements [that] include marriage, family structure, divisions of work and authority, and responsibility for the instruction of children and young people. These arrangements exist, in part, to reduce the volatility and dangers of sex—to preserve its energy, its beauty, and its pleasure; to preserve and clarify its power to join not just husband and wife to one another but parents to children, families to the community, the community to nature; to ensure, so far as possible, that the inheritors of sexuality, as they come of age, will be worthy of it.[13]

Communities maintain standards and patterns of life that encourage responsible and communally sanctioned forms of erotic bonds, with the aim of fostering the strong family ties and commitments that constitute the backbone of communal health and the conduit of culture and tradition. Communities thus chasten the absolutist claims of "rights bearers": for instance, Berry insists that they are justified in maintaining internally derived standards of decency in order to foster and maintain a desired moral ecology. He explicitly defends the communal prerogative to demand that certain books be removed from the educational curriculum and to insist on the introduction of the Bible into the classroom as "the word of God." He even reflects that "the future of community life in this country may depend on private schools and home schooling."[14] Family is the wellspring of the cultural habits and practices that foster the wisdom, judgment, and local knowledge by which humans flourish and thrive in common and rightly claim the primary role in the education and upbringing of a given community's children.

Community begins with the family but extends outward to incorporate an appropriate locus of the common good. For Berry, the common good can be achieved only in small, local settings. These dimensions cannot be precisely drawn, but Berry seems to endorse the town as the basic locus of commonweal, and the region mainly in the economic and not interpersonal realm. He is not hostile toward a conception of national or even international common good, but he recognizes that the greater scope of these larger units tends toward abstraction, which comes always at the expense of the flourishing of real human lives. Larger units than the locality or the region can flourish in the proper sense only when their constitutive parts flourish. Modern liberalism, by contrast, insists on the priority of the largest unit over the smallest, and seeks everywhere to impose a homogenous standard on a world of particularity and diversity. One sees this tendency everywhere in modern liberal society, from education to court decisions that nationalize sexual morality, from economic standardization to minute and exacting regulatory regimes.[15] The tendency of modern politics—born of a philosophy that endorses the expansion of human control—is toward the subjection of all particularities to the logic of market dynamics, exploitation of local resources, and active hostility toward diverse local customs and traditions in the name of progress and rationalism.

Modern politics, as Berry has pointed out, is impatient with local variety, particularly when it does not accept the modern embrace of material progress, economic growth, and personal liberation from all forms of work that are elemental or that forestall mobility and efficiency.[16] Berry is a strong critic of the homogenization that modern states and modern economic assumptions enforce.[17] He is a defender of "common" or "traditional" sense, that sense of the commons that often resists the logic of economic and liberal development and progress. Echoing Giambattista Vico, an early critic of the deracinated rationalism of Descartes and Hobbes, Berry defends what Vico named the *sensus communis*. Such "common knowledge" is the result of the practice and experience, the accumulated store of wisdom born of trials and corrections of people who have lived, suffered, and flourished in local settings. Rules and practices based on a preconceived notion of right cannot be imposed absent prudential consideration and respect toward common sense.[18] This is not to suggest that traditions cannot be changed or altered, but, as Burke argued, they must be given the presumptive allowance to change internally, with the understanding and assent of people who have developed lives and communities based upon those practices. There is then, in Berry's thought, a considerable respect for the dignity of "common sense," a nonexpert way of understanding the world that comes through experience, memory, and tradition, and is the source of much democratic opinion that liberalism typically dismisses.

THE DEATH OF CULTURE AND
THE RISE OF LEVIATHAN

While our main political actors argue over whether the liberal state or the market better protects the liberal citizen, they cooperate in the evisceration of actual cultures. Liberal legal structures and the market system mutually reinforce the deconstruction of cultural variety in favor of a legal and economic monoculture—or, more correctly, a mono-anticulture. Individuals, liberated and displaced from particular histories and practices, are rendered fungible within a political-economic system that requires universally replaceable parts.

Aleksandr Solzhenitsyn clearly perceived the lawlessness at the heart of liberal orders—a lawlessness that arose most centrally from liberalism's claims to value "rule of law" as it hollowed out every social norm and custom in favor of legal codes. In his controversial 1978 commencement address at Harvard University, "A World Split Apart," Solzhenitsyn criticized modern liberal reliance upon "legalistic" life. Echoing the Hobbesian and Lockean understanding of law as positivistic "hedges" constraining otherwise perfect natural autonomy, liberal legalism is posed against our natural liberty, and thus is always regarded as an imposition that otherwise should be avoided or circumvented. Delinked from any conception of "completion"—telos or flourishing—and disassociated from norms of natural law, legalism results in a widespread effort to pursue desires as fully as possible while minimally observing any legal prohibition. As Solzhenitsyn noted,

> If one is right from a legal point of view, nothing more is required, nobody may mention that one could still not be entirely right, and urge self-restraint or a renunciation of these rights, call for sacrifice and selfless risk: this would simply sound absurd. *Voluntary self-restraint is almost unheard of:* everyone strives toward further expansion to the extreme limit of legal frames.[19]

Solzhenitsyn cut to the heart of liberalism's great failing and ultimate weakness: its incapacity to foster self-governance.

It is fitting that Solzhenitsyn delivered this lecture at Harvard, the nation's premier university, since the elite universities are preeminent examples of what were once institutions of cultural formation that have become purveyors of liberal anticulture. Elite universities, and the educational system more broadly, are the front lines in the advance of liberalism's deliberate and wholesale disassembly of a broad swath of cultural norms and practices in the name of liberation from the past. Two areas in particular are served and undergirded by the educational imperative to advance the contemporary anticulture: dissolutions of sexual and economic norms, both advanced in the name of liberation of the human will that is defined especially by consumption, hedonism, and short-term thinking. The fact that each of liberalism's two main parties—"liberals" and "conservatives"—views one of these activities as problematic and the other at the core of its commitments reflects the insidiousness and pervasiveness of liberalism's advance.

The universities are the front line of the sexual revolution, the high churches charged with proselytizing the modern orthodoxy of individual liberation. As Stephen Gardner has described the central dogma of the new creed, "Eros must be raised to the level of religious cult in modern society. . . . It is in carnal desire that the modern individual believes he affirms his 'individuality.' The body must be the true 'subject' of desire because the individual must be the author of his own desire."[20] The "subject" imagined in the "state of nature" is now the resulting creature and creation of liberalism's educational system, at once claiming merely to respect the natural autonomy of individuals and actively catechizing this "normless" norm.

One of the upheavals of the sexual revolution was the rejection of long-standing rules and guidelines governing the behavior of students at the nation's colleges and universities. Formerly understood to stand in for parents—*in loco parentis*, "in place of the parent"—these institutions dictated rules regarding dormitory life, dating, curfews, visitations, and comportment. Adults—often clergy—were charged with continuing the cultivation of youth into responsible adulthood. Some fifty years after students were liberated from the nanny college, we are seeing not a sexual nirvana but widespread confusion and anarchy, and a new form of *in absentia parentis*—the paternalist state.

Long-standing local rules and cultures that governed behavior through education and cultivation of norms, manners, and morals came to be regarded as oppressive limitations on individual liberty. Those forms of control were lifted in the name of liberation, leading to regularized abuse of those liberties, born primarily of lack of any sets of practices or customs to delineate limits on behavior, especially in the fraught arena of sexual interaction. The federal government, seen as the only legitimate authority for redress, exercised its powers to reregulate the liberated behaviors. But in the wake of disassembled local cultures, there is no longer a set of norms by which to cultivate self-rule, since these would constitute an unjust limitation upon our freedom. Now there can be only punitive threats that occur after the fact. Most institutions have gotten out of the business of seeking to educate the exercise of freedom through cultivation of character and virtue; emphasis is instead placed upon the likelihood of punishment after one body has harmed another body.

This immorality tale is the Hobbesian vision in microcosm: first, tradition and culture must be eliminated as arbitrary and unjust ("natural man"). Then we see that absent such norms, anarchy ensues ("the state of nature"). Finding this anarchy unbearable, we turn to a central sovereign as our sole protector, that "Mortall God" who will protect us from ourselves ("the social contract"). We have been liberated from all custom and tradition, all authority that sought to educate within the context of ongoing communities, and have replaced these things with a distant authority that punishes us when we abuse our freedoms. And now, lacking any informal and local forms of authority, we are virtually assured that those abuses will regularly occur and that the state will find it necessary to intrude ever more minutely into personal affairs ("Prerogative").

We see an identical liberation of appetite in the economic realm, where varying economic cultures are dismantled in the name of homogenous "laws" of economics, disconnecting the pursuit of appetite from the common good, and relying upon the unreliable enforcement of abstract and distant regulation of markets, backstopped by the promise of punishment by the liberal state. Just as the destruction of distinct campus cultures and their replacement by an increasingly laissez-faire jungle with distant administrative oversight have given rise to a "rape culture," so too has "the market" replaced a world of distinctive economic cultures. The near collapse of the world economy in 2008 was, above all, the result of the elimination of a culture that existed to regulate and govern the granting and procuring of mortgages. This activity was historically understood as consummately local, requiring relationships that developed over time and in place. Laws and norms once existed to shore up the local mortgage culture, forbidding banks to open branches in communities outside those where they were based, premised on a belief that the granting and accepting of debt rested on trust and local knowledge. These laws, and the culture they supported, presupposed that "the bankers' interests and the interests of the larger community are one and the same."[21] The mortgage market was thus understood not as a naked arena of anonymous and abstract relations but as a form of organized remembrance in which trust, reputation, memory, and obligation were required for the market to operate. As J. P. Morgan chief Thomas Lamont said of his business in 1928, "the community as a whole demands of the banker that he shall be an honest observer of conditions about him, that he shall make constant and careful study of those conditions, financial, economic, social and political, and that he shall have a wide vision over them all."[22]

By 2008, the financial industry was stripped bare of any such culture rooted in nature, time and place—as were college campuses. Indeed, training at dorm parties and the fraternities of one's college were the ideal preparation for a career in the mortgage bond market, and the financial frat party of Wall Street more generally. The mortgage industry rested upon the financial equivalent of college "hookups," random encounters of strangers in which appetites (for out-sized debt or interest) were sated without any care for the consequences for the wider community. Responsibility- and cost-free loans were mutually satisfactory and wholly liberating from the constraints of an older financial order. But much as on college campuses, these arrangements led to gross irresponsibility and abuse, damaging communities and demolishing lives. The response has been the same: calls for greater government regulation and oversight over the consequences of untrammeled appetite, with threats of penalties (rarely enforced) and a massive expansion of the administrative state to oversee a basic human interaction—the effort to secure shelter. Liberation from the confinements and limitations of local market cultures brings not perfect liberty but the expansion of Leviathan. The destruction of culture achieves not liberation but powerlessness and bondage.

The dissolution of culture is simultaneously the prerequisite for the liberation of the disembedded individual, for a pervasive and encompassing market, and for the empowerment of the state. Individuals appeal to available authorities for a loosening of cultural norms and practices in the name of individual liberation, leading to various pressures that diminish or dissolve the constitutive features of long-standing informal norms. Absent these norms, individuals pursue liberalized liberty, fulfilling the desire to do as one wishes, all that is not restrained by law or causing obvious harm. But without the guiding standards of behavior that were generally developed through cultural practices and expectations, liberated individuals inevitably come into conflict. The only authority that can now adjudge those claims is the state, leading to an increase in legal and political activity in local affairs that were once generally settled by cultural norms. Liberal individualism demands the dismantling of culture; and as culture fades, Leviathan waxes and responsible liberty recedes.

PARASITIC LIBERALISM

Evidence of our anticulture surrounds us yet is pervasively denied. Liberalism extends itself by inhabiting spaces abandoned by local cultures and traditions, leading either to their discarding or suppression or, far more often, to their contentless redefinition. Rather than produce our own cultures, grounded in local places, embedded in time, and usually developed from an inheritance from relatives, neighbors, and community—music, art, storytelling, food—we are more likely to consume prepackaged, market-tested, mass-marketed consumables, often branded in commercialized symbolism that masks that culture's evisceration. A stream of stories accentuates our increasing inability to do things for ourselves, from Matthew Crawford's widely read and discussed account of the decline of shop class as an indicator of our widening ignorance of how to make and repair things to a recent report of declining sales and maintenance of pianos in the home, a consequence of the replacement of music played at home with mass-produced music.[23]

The champion of all "brood parasites" is the brown-headed cowbird, which lays its eggs in the nests of more than two hundred bird species, getting other birds to raise young cowbirds as their own. Liberalism has taken a page from this insidious practice: under liberalism, "culture" becomes a word that parasitizes the original, displacing actual cultures with a liberal simulacrum eagerly embraced by a populace that is unaware of the switch. Invocations of "culture" tend to be singular, not plural, whereas actual cultures are multiple, local, and particular. We tend to speak of such phenomena as "popular culture," a market-tested and standardized product devised by commercial enterprises and meant for mass consumption. Whereas culture is an accumulation of local and historical experience and memory, liberal "culture" is the vacuum that remains when local experience has been eviscerated, memory is lost, and every place becomes every other place. A panoply of actual cultures is replaced by celebration of "multiculturalism," the reduction of actual cultural variety to liberal homogeneity loosely dressed in easily discarded native garb. The "-ism" of "multiculturalism" signals liberalism's victorious rout of actual cultural variety. Even as cultures are replaced by a pervasive anticulture, the language of culture is advanced as a means of rendering liberal humanity's detachment from specific cultures. The homogenous celebration of every culture effectively means no culture at all. The more insistent the invocation of "pluralism" or "diversity" or, in the retail world, "choice," the more assuredly the destruction of actual cultures is advancing. Our primary allegiance is to celebration of liberal pluralism and diversity, shaping homogenized and identical adherents of difference, demanding and ensuring pervasive indifferentism.

By contrast, while cultures are many and varied, their common features almost always include a belief in the continuity between human nature and the natural world; the experience of the past and the future as embedded within the present; and assurance of the sacredness of one's place, along with depths of gratitude and responsibility to the care and preservation of one's places. Liberalism was premised upon a rejection of each of these constitutive aspects of culture, since to recognize continuity with nature, the debts and obligations attending the flow of time and generations, or a strong identity with one's place was to limit one's experience and opportunity to become a self-making author. Culture was the greatest threat to the creation of the liberal individual, and a major ambition and increasing achievement of liberalism was to reshape a world organized around the human war against nature, a pervasive amnesia about the past and indifference toward the future, and the wholesale disregard for making places worth loving and living in for generations. The replacement of these conditions with a ubiquitous and uniform anticulture is at once a crowning achievement of liberalism and among the greatest threats to our continued common life. The very basis of liberalism's success again ushers in the conditions for its demise.

CHAPTER FOUR

Technology and the Loss of Liberty

P RAISE and misgivings about our technological nature have been with us for millennia, but it is only in modern times—roughly since the dawn of the industrial era—that we have entered what we might call a technological age. While we have always been technological creatures, our reliance on technology has distinctly changed, along with our attitude toward technology and our relationship with it. One is hard-pressed to think of premodern works of poetry, literature, or song that express society-wide infatuation with technology. There are no great medieval works extolling the invention of the iron stirrup or the horse collar. Our intellectual and emotional relationship to that technology—both our wild optimism about the prospects of human progress and our profound terror about the apocalypse this same technology might bring about—are products of modern times.[1]

This oscillation between ecstasy and anxiety over technology's role in our lives has become one of the primary forms of self-expression and entertainment in the modern age, at least since Mary Shelley's novel *Frankenstein*. In recent years, the genre seems to have become even more pervasive, with an emphasis not only on technology's promise and threat but on its role in either preventing or bringing about an apocalypse. My unscientific impression is that more popular programming than ever is devoted to this theme. If our sense of threat from nuclear weapons seems to have waned somewhat, we have found other night terrors, from medical catastrophe to cyborg warfare on humanity to cataclysmic climate change and the specter of human extinction.

Over the past few decades, several blockbuster films have depicted the apocalypse as the result of uncontrollable forces that humans valiantly combatted, often successfully. The threats include extinction by asteroid, as in *Armageddon* and *Deep Impact*; alien invasion, as in *Independence Day*, *War of the Worlds*, and *Battle Los Angeles*; and, in 2012, general demise coincident with the end of the Mayan calendar. In all of these films, it is technology, in various ways, that is the source of humanity's eventual triumph over or salvation from these threats.

But most recent entrants to the genre seem rather to focus on how our technology is likely to be the *source* of our doom. Some recent films hark back to fears of a nuclear apocalypse, such as *The Book of Eli* or *The Road*. Others posit that we will end civilization through global warming, such as *The Day after Tomorrow*. There are films about medical experiments going awry, leading to a massive die-off, such as *I Am Legend*, *Quarantine*, *Contagion*, and *Rise of the Planet of the Apes*. There are stories about our technology failing or attacking us, such as the Terminator series and, more recently, the television show *Revolution*, about a time when all machines cease to operate and electricity ceases to flow. The successful HBO series *Westworld* depicts machines becoming more human than a dehumanized humanity, intimating that we may have invented a better version of ourselves. Similarly, the digital series *H+* tells of a future in which developments in nanotechnology lead to widespread implantation of tiny chips into human beings, allowing them to discard cellphones, tablets, and computers by becoming interconnected receivers of data, texts, and email. While the series begins with triumphalist pronouncements by transhumanist techno-optimists, the technology soon turns deadly, causing a massive die-off of millions who have been implanted.

Most examples of this recent genre seems to reflect a widespread foreboding about a shared sense of powerlessness, and even the potential for a new kind of bondage to the very technology that is supposed to liberate us. These movies and programs portray how, in our optimistic and even hubristic belief that our technology will usher in a new age of freedom, we discover in various ways that we are subjects to those very technologies. Far from controlling our technology for our own betterment, we find that the technology ends up either ruling or destroying us.

ANDROID HUMANITY

A host of academic studies and works also explore, if less dramatically, the ways in which we are subjects to the transformative effects of our technologies. A paramount example today may be found in anxious descriptions of how the internet and social media are inescapably changing us, mainly for the worse. Several recent books and studies describing the measurable baleful effects of these technologies have found a ready audience well beyond the usual academic circles. For instance, in his widely discussed book *The Shallows*, Nicholas Carr describes how the internet is literally changing us, transforming our brains into different organs from those of the preinternet world. Appealing to developments in studies of brain plasticity, Carr describes how persistent occupation with the internet is leading to physiological changes to our brains, and hence to the ways we think, learn, and act. He argues that sustained exposure to the internet is rewiring our synapses, making us intensely hungry for frequent changes in images and content and less able than our forebears to concentrate and focus. For Carr, this change is not altogether for the worse, since some areas of the brain have shown measurable increases, particularly those related to decision making and problem solving. But those gains are accompanied by significant losses in language facility, memory, and concentration. We are, he argues, becoming more shallow, not simply in a superficial way, but physiologically. The internet is making us dumber.[2]

Other books emphasize the contributions of the internet and the social media to changes in our social and relational lives, often for the worse. In her book *Alone Together* MIT's Sherry Turkle assembles evidence that our pervasive use of modern social media doesn't so much create new communities as it substitutes for the real-world communities that it destroys. Turkle reminds us that the root of the word "community" means literally "to give among each other" and argues that such a practice requires "physical proximity" and "shared responsibilities." The growing presence of social media fosters relationships that avoid either of these constitutive elements of community, replacing that thicker set of shared practices with the thinner and more evanescent bonds of "networks." Turkle is not simply nostalgic—she acknowledges the difficult and even awful aspects of community in earlier times. She describes the community in which her grandparents lived, for instance, as "rife with deep antagonisms." But the same thickness that gave rise to such contentious relations, she writes, also inspired people to take care of each other in times of need. Turkle fears that we are losing not only that experience but also the capacity to form the thick bonds that constitute community, and that our attraction to social media at once undermines these bonds and provides a pale simulacrum to fill the void. Social media become ersatz substitutes for what they destroy, and Turkle seems pessimistic about the prospects for slowing this transformation. At best we can try to limit our children's access to the internet, but Turkle seems resigned to dim prospects of fundamentally changing the current dynamic.³

These recent works follow in the tradition established by critics of technology who emphasize the way that technology changes us and, in particular, destroys long-standing ways of life, attacking the very basis of culture. There is a long tradition of cultural criticism, ranging from Lewis Mumford's critiques of modernism to Jacques Ellul's *The Technological Society*, which emphasizes the way the "technique" of technology erases everything in its path in the name of utility and efficiency, and more recently to Wendell Berry, who has argued that machine technology has its own logic, which tends to destroy the practices and traditions of a community. Perhaps the most representative voice in this tradition is that of Neil Postman, whose book *Technopoly*—published in 1992—was suggestively subtitled *The Surrender of Culture to Technology*.

In that book, Postman describes the rise in the modern era of what he calls Technocracy. Preindustrial forms of culture and social organization used tools no less than technocratic societies, Postman writes, but the tools they employed "did not attack (or more precisely, were not intended to attack) the dignity and integrity of the culture into which they were introduced. With some exceptions, tools did not prevent people from believing in their traditions, in their God, in their politics, in their methods of education, or in the legitimacy of their social organization."[4] The tools adopted by a Technocracy, by contrast, constantly transform the way of life. Postman writes, "Everything must give way, in some degree, to their development. . . . Tools are not integrated into the culture; they attack the culture. They bid to *become* the culture. As a consequence, tradition, social mores, myth, politics, ritual, and religion have to fight for their lives."[5] From technocracy we have entered the age of "technopoly," in which a culturally flattened world operates under an ideology of progress that leads to "the submission of all forms of cultural life to the sovereignty of technique and technology." The residual cultural practices that survived the era of technocracy now give way to a transformed world in which technology is itself our culture—or anticulture, a tradition-destroying and custom-undermining dynamic that replaces cultural practices, memory, and beliefs.

What these critiques have in common is the supposition that our technology is changing us, often for the worse. We are the subjects of its activity and largely powerless before its transformative power. Our anxiety arises from the belief that we may no longer control the technology that is supposed to be a main tool of our liberty.

Perhaps an even deeper anxiety arises from the belief that there is an inevitability to technological advances that no amount of warning about their dangers can prevent. A kind of Hegelian or Darwinian narrative seems to dominate our worldview. We seem inescapably to be either creating our own destroyer or, as Lee Silver writes in *Remaking Eden*, evolving into a fundamentally different creature that we have reason to fear becoming. Our popular culture seems to be a kind of electronic Cassandra, seeing the future but unable to get anyone to believe it. The culture offers entertaining prophecies born of our anxieties, and we take perverse pleasure distracting ourselves with portrayals of our powerlessness.

One example of this genre of technological (as well as political) inevitability, albeit framed in a triumphalist mode, is the narrative advanced by Francis Fukuyama in his famous essay, and later book, *The End of History*. The book, in particular, provides a long materialist explanation of the inescapable scientific logic, driven by the need for constant advances in military technology, contributing to the ultimate rise of the liberal state. Only the liberal state, in Fukuyama's view, could provide the environment for the open scientific inquiry that has led to the greatest advances in military devices and tactics. All others are inexorably forced to follow. Yet, in a book written only a decade later on advances in biotechnology and "our posthuman future," Fukuyama acknowledges that this very logic might end up altering human nature itself, and as a result imperiling the political order of liberal democracy it had been developed to support.[6]

Other works speak of technological inevitability as a result of forces embedded within the nature of reality itself. In his now-classic 1967 essay "Do Machines Make History?" the economic historian Robert Heilbroner depicts a logic within the development of history that pushed humans toward technological development. While societies might adopt those technologies at different speeds, nevertheless there is a form of "soft determinism" in technological development. Perhaps more forthright still is the argument found in Daniel J. Boorstin's short book *The Republic of Technology*, published in 1978, in which he depicts technological development as following a kind of "Law" like that of gravity or thermodynamics. For example, "the Supreme Law of the Republic of Technology is convergence, the tendency for everything to become more like everything else."[7] The laws governing technological development thus inevitably shape our human world in an increasingly identical form—anticipating today's suspicions that modern technology's child, "globalization," is a kind of inescapable unfolding.

Whether told as praise or lament, this narrative of inevitability tends to grant autonomy to technology itself, as if its advances occurred independently of human intention and thought. It becomes a process inescapably driven by its own internal logic—or, to modify a phrase of Hegel's, "the cunning of techne," the unconscious unfolding of a technological Geist that leads inevitably to convergence and singularity, a fully technologized culmination of History with a capital H. It, too, perhaps has a slaughterbench that demands its share of victims in the course of its unfolding, but their sacrifice is justified by Progress to a better and even perfected future.

I want to challenge, or at least complicate, these two related ways that modern humans have come to discern and portray technology—as something that shapes and even remakes us, and does so with a kind of iron law of inevitability. Doing so requires me to take a step back into an exploration of what Aristotle called "the master science" of all sciences—political philosophy—and try to discern the deeper origins of humanity's new relationship to technology.

THE TECHNOLOGY OF LIBERALISM

As I have argued throughout, liberalism above all advances a new understanding of liberty. In the ancient world—whether pre-Christian antiquity, particularly ancient Greece, or during the long reign of Christendom—the dominant definition of liberty involved recognition that it required an appropriate form of self-governance. This conception of liberty was based upon a reciprocal relationship between the self-government of individuals through the cultivation of virtue (whether ancient or Christian conceptions of virtue, which differed), and the self-government of polities, in which the governing aspiration was the achievement of the common good. Ancient thought sought a "virtuous circle" of polities that would support the fostering of virtuous individuals, and of virtuous individuals who would form the civic life of a polity oriented toward the common good. Much of the challenge faced by ancient thinkers was how to start such a virtuous circle where it did not exist or existed only partially, and how to maintain it against the likelihood of civic corruption and persistent temptation to vice.

Liberty, by this understanding, was not doing as one wished, but was choosing the right and virtuous course. To be free, above all, was to be free from enslavement to one's own basest desires, which could never be fulfilled, and the pursuit of which could only foster ceaseless craving and discontent. Liberty was thus the condition achieved by self-rule, over one's own appetites and over the longing for political dominion.

The defining feature of modern thought was the rejection of this definition of liberty in favor of the one more familiar to us today. Liberty, as defined by the originators of modern liberalism, was the condition in which humans were completely free to pursue whatever they desired. This condition—fancifully conceived as a "state of nature," was imagined as a condition before the creation of political society, a condition of pure liberty. Its opposite was thus conceived as constraint. Liberty was no longer, as the ancients held, the condition of just and appropriate self-rule.

The main political obstacle to be overcome was limitation upon individual liberty imposed by other people. The old political orders, previously devoted to the inculcation of virtue and the commendation of the common good, were attacked early on by Niccolò Machiavelli as "imaginary republics and principalities," dealing in *oughts* rather than taking humans as they actually are. In order to unleash the productive and scientific capacity of human societies, a different mode and order had to be introduced—a completely new form of political technology that made possible a technological society. That form of technology was the modern republic—posited on the rejection of the key premises of ancient republicanism—and above all it rested on the harnessing of self-interest in both the public and the private realms in order to secure human liberty and increase the scope, scale, and extent of human power over nature.

The precondition of our technological society was that great achievement of political technology, the "applied technology" of liberal theory, our Constitution. The Constitution is the embodiment of a set of modern principles that sought to overturn ancient teachings and shape a distinctly different modern human. It is a kind of precursor technology, the precondition for the technology that today seems to govern us. According to James Madison in *Federalist* 10, the first object of government is the protection of "the diversity in the faculties of men," which is to say our individual pursuits and the outcomes of those pursuits—particularly, Madison notes, differences in attainment of property. Government exists to protect the greatest possible sphere of individual liberty, and it does so by encouraging the pursuit of self-interest among both the citizenry and public servants. "Ambition must be made to counteract ambition": powers must be separate and divided powers to prevent any one person from centralizing and seizing power; but at the same time, the government itself is to be given substantial new powers to act directly on individuals, both to liberate them from the constraints of their particular localities, and to promote the expansion of commerce and the "useful arts and sciences."

This new political technology developed to expand the practice of the modern understanding of liberty was designed to liberate us from partial loyalties to particular people and places, and make us into individuals who, above all, strive to achieve our individual ambitions and desires. Part of the new technology of modern republicanism is what Madison calls an "enlarged orbit" that will increase individual prospects for their ambitions while making our interpersonal ties and commitments more tenuous. One of the ways modern republicanism was intended to combat the ancient problem of political faction was not by commending public spiritedness but by fostering a "mistrust of motives" that would result from the large expanse of the republic, constantly changing political dynamics, the encouragement to "pluralism" and expansion of diversity as a default preference, and thus the shifting commitments of the citizenry. A technological society like our own comes into being through a new kind of political technology—one that replaces the ancient commendation of virtue and aspiration to the common good with self-interest, the unleashed ambition of individuals, an emphasis on private pursuits over a concern for public weal, and an acquired ability to reconsider any relationships that limit our personal liberty. In effect, a new political technology is invented—a "new science of politics"—that itself conditions our understanding of the purposes and ends of science and technology. Technology does not exist autonomous of political and social norms and beliefs, but its development and applications are shaped by such norms. Liberalism introduces a set of norms that lead us, ironically, to the belief that technology develops independent of any norms and intentions, but rather shapes our norms, our polity, and even humanity, and inevitably escapes our control.

In light of this set of political preconditions to a technological society, we can reconsider the two dominant narratives by which we tend to think about our relationship to technology: that technology "shapes" us in ways that should cause regret and even concern, and that its effects are inevitable and irreversible.

First, as we have seen, there is much concern about the ways that modern technology undermines community and tends to make us more individualistic, but in light of the deeper set of conditions that led to the creation of our technological society, we can see that "technology" simply supports the fundamental commitments of early-modern political philosophy and its founding piece of technology, our modern republican government and the constitutional order. It is less a matter of our technology "making us" than of our deeper political commitments shaping our technology. You could say that our political technology is the operating system that creates the environment in which various technological programs may thrive, and that the operating system was itself the result of a transformation of the definition and understanding of liberty.

This recognition was acknowledged, if incompletely, in a widely discussed article that appeared in the *Atlantic* entitled "Is Facebook Making Us Lonely?" Its author, Stephen Marche, begins in the usual manner, showing how a form of technology—Facebook in this case—appears to be contributing to greater instances of loneliness and corresponding feelings of sadness and even depression. The author views loneliness as a nearly pathological condition, rising to epidemic levels even as the use of social networking tools like Facebook has increased. Some 20 percent of Americans—sixty million people—say they experience unhappiness due to loneliness, he reports, and a vast array of therapeutic social services has arisen to attempt to combat this form of depression. "A matter of nostalgic lament has morphed into an issue of public health."[8]

Yet, Marche refreshingly avoids *blaming* Facebook for this epidemic of loneliness. Rather, he notes that Facebook, and technologies like it, have facilitated or even enabled a preexisting predilection—the long-standing American desire to be independent and free. Facebook is thus a tool that elicits loneliness from a deeper set of philosophical, political, and even theological commitments. As Marche points out, "Loneliness is one of the first things that Americans spend their money achieving. . . . We are lonely because we want to be lonely. We have made ourselves lonely." Technologies like Facebook, he writes, "are the by-product of a long-standing national appetite for independence." That appetite, as I have argued, is itself the result of a redefinition of the nature of liberty.

Consider a different kind of "technology": how we inhabit the world through our built environment. More than any other people, Americans have pursued a living arrangement that promotes the conception of ourselves as independent and apart, primarily through the creation of the postwar suburb, made possible by the technology of the automobile. The suburb, however, was not simply the "creation" of the automobile; rather, the automobile and its accessories—highways, gas stations, shopping malls, fast-food chains—permitted a life-style that Americans, because of their deeper philosophical commitments, were predisposed to prefer. We find other evidence of such precommitments beyond the automobile's influence, such as the transformation of building styles documented in the architectural historian Richard Thomas's remarkable 1975 article "From Porch to Patio." Thomas describes a striking postwar transition in house styles in which the front porch, formerly the most prominent feature in the elevation of a house, disappeared in favor of a patio tucked behind the house. He describes the social and even civic role played by the porch—not only offering cooler temperatures and a breeze in the era before air-conditioning, but providing "intermediate spaces," a kind of civil space, between the private world of the house and the public spaces of the sidewalk and street. The front porch, often sited within easy chatting distance of the sidewalk, was an architectural reflection of an era with a high expectation of sociability among neighbors. The back patio gained in popularity around the same time as the increased use of the automobile and the rise of the suburb—all of which created a built environment conducive to privacy, apartness, insularity, and a declining commitment to social and civic spaces and practices. These technologies reflected the commitments of modern republican liberty, but they did not—as is too often thought—make us "lonely."[9]

As a counterexample, one could pose social and cultural norms that govern the use of technology for different purposes and ends. The old-order Amish are often regarded as a society with a phobia toward technology, but this view reflects a preliminary misunderstanding of technology—in particular, an incapacity to recognize that the technology that is adopted by that culture reflects a prior commitment to certain social ends, just as liberal adoption of technology seeks to effect its own distinctive ends. Some of the decisions of the Amish—like their rejection of zippers—are incomprehensible to many of us, but what is most of interest is the basic criterion they use to decide whether to adopt, and more important how to adopt, technology in their society. All technological developments are subject to the basic question, "Will this or won't it help support the fabric of our community?" It is believed that the automobile and electricity will not (though propane-powered implements are approved). To me, one of the most powerful examples of this criterion is the decision to eschew insurance, on the grounds that our form of insurance is premised on maximum anonymity and minimal personal commitment. For the price of a premium based on calculations of actuarial tables, I join a pool with others seeking insurance for a variety of objects or conditions, such as automobile, house, life, or health. When one of these areas suffers damage, I (or my heirs) can turn to the insurance company for some compensatory payment to make me whole again. The funds are drawn from the pool to which all the insured contributed, but we all remain wholly unaware of how, and to whom, payments are made. I am insured against a variety of tragedies but wholly off the hook for any personal responsibility or obligation to anyone else in the insurance pool. My only obligation is a financial transaction with the company providing the insurance.

Certain Amish communities ban members from purchasing insurance. Rather, the community itself is their "insurance pool": members seek to foster a community where it is everyone's shared responsibility and obligation to make someone who suffers a loss "whole" again.[10] As the economist Stephen Marglin writes in his insightful book *The Dismal Science: How Thinking Like an Economist Undermines Community*, "The Amish, perhaps unique in twentieth-century America in their attention to fostering community, forbid insurance precisely because they understand that the market relationship between an individual and the insurance company undermines the mutual dependence of the individuals. For the Amish, barn raisings are not exercises in nostalgia, but the cement that binds the community together."[11]

I note this profound difference of approach to the question and use of technology between the likes of the old-order Amish and contemporary liberals not to urge that denizens of liberal modernity adopt wholesale the practices and beliefs of the Amish but to make a specific point. We regard our condition as one of freedom, whereas from the standpoint of liberal modernity, adherents of Amish culture are widely perceived to be subject to oppressive rules and customs. Yet we should note that while we have choices about what kind of technology we will use—whether a sedan or a jeep, an iPhone or a Galaxy, a Mac or a PC—we largely regard ourselves as subject to the logic of technological development and ultimately not in a position to eschew any particular technology. By contrast, the Amish—who seem to constrain so many choices—exercise choice over the use and adoption of technologies based upon criteria upon which they base their community. Who is free?

In our remaking of the world—through obvious technologies like the internet, and less obvious but no less influential ones like insurance—we embrace and deploy technologies that make us how we imagine ourselves being. And in a profound irony, it is precisely in this quest to attain ever-more-perfect individual liberty and autonomy that we increasingly suspect that we might fundamentally lack choice about adoption of those technologies.

To secure our modern form of freedom through the great modern technology of the liberal political order and the capitalist economic system it fosters, we ceaselessly need to increase our power and expand the empire of liberty. Concentrations of political and economic power are necessary for ever-increasing individual liberty. In contradiction to our contemporary political discourse, which suggests that there is some conflict between the individual and centralized power, we need to understand that ever-expanding individual liberty is actually the creation of a sprawling and intricate set of technologies that, while liberating the individual from the limitations of both nature and obligation, leave us feeling increasingly powerless, voiceless, alone—and unfree.

This is felt keenly, and with ultimate irony, in the growing belief that we no longer control the objects or the trajectory of our technological world. As early as 1978, Daniel Boorstin wrote in *The Republic of Technology* that "technology creates its own momentum and is irreversible," and that "we live, and will live, in a world of increasingly involuntary commitments."[12] By this he meant that we will no longer choose our technologies but will be inescapably drawn to those that make us ever more the creatures imagined by Hobbes and Locke in the State of Nature: autonomous, free, yet subjects of the very technologies that allow us the feeling of independence. Rather than being chosen, our technologies will arise from a dynamic we no longer control, and further enlarge a system over which we have only the faintest grasp. If our airwaves are increasingly filled with dramas about a technological apocalypse, many of those also posit a shadowy and unknown distant power that seems to pull the strings even when we think we are autonomous. Think of *The Matrix*, that quasi-Platonic film that put into image the suspicion that we are prisoners in a cave whose images are controlled by puppeteers, but which we believe to be reality itself.

Maybe the deepest irony is that our capacity for self-government has waned almost to the point of nonexistence. In our current lamentations about a variety of crises—the civic crisis in which we seem to have lost the capacity to speak the language of common good; our financial crisis, in which both public and private debt, accrued for immediate satiation, is foisted upon future generations in the vague hope that they will devise a way to deal with it; our environmental crisis, in which most of the answers to our problems are framed in terms of technological fixes but which ultimately require us to control our ceaseless appetites; and the moral crisis of a society in which personal commitments such as families so easily unravel and are replaced by therapy and social programs—we fail to see the deep commonalities arising from the very success of our modern liberal project. We are certainly right to congratulate ourselves for the successes of our technology, but we are also right to worry about the costs of our technological society. Our "culture of technology" was premised, from the very start, on a false definition of liberty, and it now seems to be leading us ineluctably into a condition of bondage to the consequences of our own fantasy.

CHAPTER FIVE

Liberalism against Liberal Arts

EFORE the advent of liberalism, culture was the most pervasive human technology and the fundamental locus of education. It was the comprehensive shaping force of the person who took part in, and would in turn pass on, the deepest commitments of a civilization. As the word itself intimates, a culture cultivates; it is the soil in which the human person grows and—if it is a good culture—flourishes.

But if liberalism ultimately replaces all forms of culture with a pervasive anticulture, then it must undermine education as well. In particular, it must undermine liberal education, the education that was understood as the main means of educating free persons by means of deep engagement with the fruits of long cultural inheritance, particularly the great texts of antiquity and the long Christian tradition. To the extent that a fully realized liberalism undermines culture and cultivation into liberty as a form of self-governance, an education for a free people is displaced by an education that makes liberal individuals servants to the end of untutored appetite, restlessness, and technical mastery of the natural world. Liberal education is replaced with servile education.

Liberalism undermines liberal education in the first instance by detaching the educational enterprise itself from culture and making it an engine of anticulture. Education must be insulated from the shaping force of culture as the exercise of living within nature and a tradition, instead stripped bare of any cultural specificity in the name of a cultureless multiculturalism, an environmentalism barren of a formative encounter with nature, and a monolithic and homogenous "diversity." Its claims to further multiculturalism only distract from its pervasive anticultural and homogenizing impetus.

Liberalism further undermines education by replacing a definition of liberty as an education in self-government with liberty as autonomy and the absence of constraint. Ultimately it destroys liberal education, since it begins with the assumption that we are born free, rather than that we must learn to become free. Under liberalism, the liberal arts are instruments of personal liberation, an end that is consistently pursued in the humanities, in the scientific and mathematical disciplines (STEM), and in economics and business. In the humanities, liberatory movements based on claims of identity regard the past as a repository of oppression, and hence displace the legitimacy of the humanities as a source of education. Meanwhile, the subjects that advance the practical and effectual experience of autonomy—STEM, economics, and business—come to be regarded as the sole subjects of justified study. The classical understanding of liberal arts as aimed at educating the free human being is displaced by emphasis upon the arts of the private person. An education fitting for a *res publica* is replaced with an education suited for a *res idiotica*—in the Greek, a "private" and isolated person. The purported difference between left and right disappears as both concur that the sole legitimate end of education is the advance of power through the displacement of the liberal arts.

LIBERALISM'S ATTACK ON LIBERAL ARTS

The phrase "liberal arts" contains the same root as the word "liberty." The liberal arts have their origins in a premodern world, hence are rooted in a premodern understanding of liberty. We who are the heirs of the liberal tradition are conditioned to believe in a definition of liberty that equates with the absence of external constraint. The social contract theories of thinkers like Hobbes and Locke, who defined the natural condition of human beings as one of prepolitical liberty, tell us that we begin as creatures who are free, and we submit to the external and artificial contrivance of law only in order to achieve a measure of security and social peace. In Locke's understanding, we submit to law in order to "secure" our liberty and "dispose of [our] possessions or persons as [we] see fit."

The liberal arts precede this understanding of liberty. They reflect, instead, a premodern understanding—one found in the teachings of such authors as Plato, Aristotle, and Cicero, and in the biblical and Christian traditions, articulated not only in the Bible but in the works of Augustine, Aquinas, Dante, More, and Milton. It is no coincidence that at the heart of the liberal arts tradition was an emphasis on classical and Christian texts by these authors. For all their many differences, they all agree that liberty is not a condition into which we are naturally born but one we achieve through habituation, training, and education—particularly the discipline of self-command. It is the result of a long process of learning. Liberty is the learned capacity to govern oneself using the higher faculties of reason and spirit through the cultivation of virtue. The condition of doing as one wants is defined in this premodern view as one of slavery, in which we are driven by our basest appetites to act against our better nature. It was the central aim of the liberal arts to cultivate the free person and the free citizen, in accordance with this understanding of liberty. The liberal arts *made* us free.

For many years, this conception of knowledge lay at the heart of liberal education. It derived its authority from the faith traditions and cultural practices that one generation sought to pass on to the next. One sees it today on most campuses as a palimpsest, a medieval vellum whose old writing was erased to make room for new writing, but from which a trained eye can still read the ancient teaching. In the gothic buildings, the name "professor," "dean," and "provost," the flowing robes that are ceremonially donned once or twice a year—these and some other presences are fragments of an older tradition, once the animating spirit of these institutions, now mostly dead on most campuses.

One sees this older tradition—evidence of this palimpsest—perhaps most vividly in the aspirational mottos and symbolic seals that educational institutions adopted as goals for themselves and their students. One representative motto is that of Ohio University in Athens, Ohio, which was founded as

American University in 1804, one of the first universities in what was then the unsettled West. Its original motto is still found on the university seal: *Religio, Doctrina, Civilitas, prae omnibus Virtus:* Religion, true learning, civility; above all, virtue. On the Class Gateway on one of the main approaches to campus is inscribed a sentence taken verbatim from the Northwest Ordinance of 1787: "Religion, morality, and knowledge being necessary to good government and the happiness of mankind, schools and the means of education shall forever be encouraged." These sentiments guided the founding of the nation's public universities, which, in addition to contributing to the advance of science and practical knowledge, were above all charged with fostering virtue and morality.

Another public university, the University of Texas at Austin, has emblazoned on its seal the motto *Disciplina Praesidium Civitate*, which is translated as "A cultivated mind is the guardian genius of democracy." These words are drawn from a statement by Texas's second president, Mirabeau Lamar: "A cultivated mind is the guardian genius of democracy and, while guided and controlled by virtue, the noblest attribute of man. It is the only dictator that freemen acknowledge and the only security that freemen desire." This fuller statement, with its stress on the relationship of virtue, authority, and liberty, and with the overtones in the word *disciplina* not only of "cultivation" but of discipline, points to the conception of liberty as the achievement of hard-won self-control through the discipline of virtue. The image on the seal includes an open book on the shield's upper field, showing the means by which this discipline of liberty is to be won: through education in the wisdom, the lessons, and the cautions of the past. The aim of such an education is not "critical thinking" but the achievement of liberty governed by the discipline of virtue.

As these mottos attest, the older tradition sought to foster an ethic of restraint. It recognized that humankind was singular among the creatures in its capacity to choose among numerous options, and so in its need for guidance in that condition of liberty. This liberty, the ancients understood, was subject to misuse and excess: the oldest stories in our tradition, including the story of humankind's fall from Eden, told of the human propensity to use freedom badly. The goal of understanding ourselves was to understand how to use our liberty well, especially how to govern appetites that seemed inherently insatiable. At the heart of the liberal arts in this older tradition was an education in what it meant to be human, above all how to achieve freedom, not only from external restraint but from the tyranny of internal appetite and desire. The "older science" sought to encourage the hard and difficult task of negotiating what was permitted and what was forbidden, what constituted the highest and best use of our freedom, and what actions were wrong. Each new generation was encouraged to consult the great works of our tradition, the epics, the great tragedies and comedies, the reflections of philosophers and theologians, the revealed word of God, the countless books that sought to teach us how to use our liberty well. To be free—*liberal*—was an *art*, something learned not by nature or instinct but by refinement and education. And the soul of the liberal arts was the humanities, education in how to be a human being.

The collapse of the liberal arts in this nation follows closely upon the redefinition of liberty, away from its ancient and Christian understanding of self-rule and disciplined self-command, in favor of an understanding of liberty as the absence of restraints upon one's desires. If the purpose of the liberal arts was to seek an instruction in self-rule, then its teaching no longer aligns with the contemporary ends of education. Long-standing requirements to learn ancient languages in order to read the classical texts, or to require an intimate familiarity with the Bible and scriptural interpretation, were displaced by a marketplace of studies driven by individual taste and preference. Above all, the liberal arts are increasingly replaced by "STEM," which combines a remnant of the ancient liberal arts—science and mathematics—with their applied forms, technology and engineering, alongside increasing demands for preparation for careers in business and finance.

The American university slowly changed from the teaching of this older science to a teaching of the new. In the nineteenth century, a growing number of universities were established or began to emulate the example of the German universities, dividing themselves into specialized disciplines and placing a new stress upon the education of graduate students—a training in expert knowledge—and placed a new priority upon discovery of new knowledge. Slowly the religious underpinnings of the university were discarded and discontinued; while the humanities continued to remain at the heart of the liberal arts education, they were no longer guided by a comprehensive vision afforded by the religious traditions whose vision and creed had provided the organizing principle for the efforts of the university. In the middle part of the twentieth century, renewed emphasis upon scientific training and technological innovation—spurred especially by government investment in the "useful arts and sciences"—further reoriented many of the priorities of the university system.

Liberal education came to be seen as irrelevant for the pursuit of modern liberty, particularly as understood as that liberty secured by military power, science, and technology, and the expansion of capitalist markets to every corner of the globe. The idea of the university was passing out of existence, declared the chancellor of the University of California, Clark Kerr, in his 1963 Godkin Lectures, published later as *The Uses of the University*. In place of a form of education that was guided by a teleological or religious vision of what constituted an education of the best human being, he announced the inevitable rise of the multiversity, a massive organization that would be driven above all by the radical separations of the endeavors of the various members of the university aimed at providing useful knowledge to the military and industrial demands of the nation. He declared that "the multiversity was central to the further industrialization of the nation, to spectacular increases in productivity with affluence following, to the substantial extension of human life, and to worldwide military and scientific supremacy."[1] The aim of the new "multiversity" was to advance the Baconian project of human mastery over the world.

Following upon this redefinition of the aims of the university, the incentives and motivations of the faculty were brought increasingly into accord with new science's imperative to create new knowledge: faculty training would emphasize the creation of original work, and tenure would be achieved through the publication of a corpus of such work and the approval of far-flung experts in a faculty member's field who would attest to the originality and productivity of the work. A market in faculty hiring and recruitment was born. Faculty ceased to be committed to particular institutions, their missions, and even their students, and instead increasingly understood themselves to be members of a profession. Moral formation ceased to be a relevant criterion in one's job description; such concerns were not only irrelevant to professional success but opposed to modern notions of liberty.

The university structure was reoriented to stress innovation and the creation of "new knowledge." The guiding imperative of education became progress, not an education in liberty derived from a deep engagement with the past. One can valuably contrast the commitments of the seal designed at the time of the founding of the University of Texas with the mission statement devised in more recent years and found on the main web portal of the university.[2] Articulated beneath a picture of the old seal—following the obligatory verbiage about a dedication to "excellence" in education—one finds a statement about the contemporary purpose. The current mission of the university is "the advancement of society through research, creative activity, scholarly inquiry and the development of new knowledge." The stress in this updated mission statement is upon the research and scientific mission of the university, notably the aim of creating "new knowledge," not "the cultivated mind that is guided by virtue." One searches in vain for a modern rearticulation of the sentiments of the older motto; one finds, rather than the inculcation of virtue, only the emphasis upon research in the service of progress—

particularly that progress that contributes to that centuries-old ambition to subject nature to human will. This change of emphasis is to be found in the updated mission statement of nearly every university in America.

As a practical effect, the insistence by students no longer to be required to take a sequential education in the liberal arts, in the belief that they should sooner begin study of something "practical," aligns perfectly with the interest of faculty to focus on the "creation of new knowledge" and the concomitant focus on research and graduate students. Students and faculty alike mutually abandon a focus on the liberal arts, essentially out of the same imperative: service to the conception of freedom at the heart of the liberal order. Amid their freedom, students increasingly feel that they have no choice but to pursue the most practical major, eschewing subjects to which native curiosity might attract them in obeisance to the demands of the market. Unsurprisingly, the number of majors in the humanities continues to decline precipitously, and a growing number of schools are eliminating disciplines that are no longer attractive within the university marketplace.

Those best positioned to defend the role of the humanities at the heart of the liberal arts—members of the professoriate—on the one hand lament this collapse but blame it on administrators and "neoliberalism." They fail to see how the treatment of the humanities is more deeply a reflection of the liberal order than a stance of resistance. The professoriate in the liberal arts has failed to contest, let alone resist, the dominant liberal trends because of a pervasive incapacity to correctly diagnose the source of the forces arrayed against the liberal arts.

Humanities and more humanistic social science faculty—predominantly progressive—sought instead to conform the liberal arts to dominant liberal subcurrents, mainly by turning against the very thing they studied, the "great books," and calling for a stance of progressive interrogation of the object being studied. Conservative faculty largely opposed the campus left by demanding devotion to the study of the Great Books without recognizing that many of these books were the source of the very forces displacing the study of old books. Both sides allowed the liberal transformation of the academy to proceed unopposed.

The left's answer was unexamined acquiescence. In response to these tectonic shifts, those who labored in the humanities began to question their place within the university. Their practitioners still studied the great texts, but the reason for doing so was increasingly in doubt.[3] Did it make sense any longer to teach young people the challenging lessons of how to use freedom well, when the scientific world was soon to make those lessons unnecessary? Could an approach based on culture and tradition remain relevant in an age that valued, above all, innovation and progress? How could the humanities prove their worth in the eyes of administrators and the broader world?

These doubts within the humanities were a fertile seedbed for self-destructive tendencies. Inspired by Heideggerian theories that placed primacy on the liberation of the will, first poststructuralism and then postmodernism took root. These and other approaches, while apparently hostile to the rationalist claims of the sciences, were embraced out of the need to conform to the academic demands, set by the natural sciences, for "progressive" knowledge. Faculty could demonstrate their progressiveness by showing the backwardness of the texts; they could "create knowledge" by showing their superiority to the authors they studied; they could display their antitraditionalism by attacking the very books that were the basis of their discipline. Philosophies that preached "the hermeneutics of suspicion," that aimed to expose the way texts were deeply informed by inegalitarian prejudices, and that even questioned the idea that texts contained a "teaching" as intended by the author, offered the humanities the possibility of proving themselves relevant in the terms set by the modern scientific approach.[4] By adopting a jargon comprehensible only to "experts," they could emulate the scientific priesthood, even if by doing so they betrayed the humanities' original mandate to guide students through their cultural inheritance. Professors in the humanities showed their worth by destroying the thing they studied.[5]

In an effort to keep pace with their counterparts in STEM disciplines, the humanities became the most conspicuously liberative of the disciplines, even challenging (albeit fecklessly) the legitimacy of the scientific enterprise. Natural conditions—such as those inescapably linked to the biological facts of human sexuality—came to be regarded as "socially constructed." Nature was no longer a standard in any sense, since it was now manipulable. Why accept any of the facts of biology when those "facts" could be altered, when identity itself is a matter of choice? If humans had any kind of "nature," then the sole permanent feature that seemed acceptable was the centrality of will—the raw assertion of power over restraints or limits, and the endless possibilities of self-creation.

Ironically, while postmodernism has posed itself as the great opponent of rationalist scientism, it shares the same basic impulse: both rose to dominance in the university in conformity with the modern definition of freedom. In the humanities, this belief today takes the form of radical emancipatory theory focused on destroying all forms of hierarchy, tradition, and authority, liberating the individual through the tools of research and progress. A special focus of the modern academy is sexual autonomy, a pursuit that reveals how closely it ultimately sides with a scientific project aimed at mastering all aspects of nature, including human reproduction.[6] The humanities and social sciences also focus on identity politics and redressing past injustices to specific groups, under the "multicultural" and "diversity" banners that ironically contribute to a campus monoculture. The groups that are deemed worthy of strenuous efforts to redress grievances are identified for features relating to their bodies—race, gender, sexual identity—while "communities of work and culture," including cohesive ethnic and class groupings, receive scant attention. Thus while students' groups grounded in racial or sexual identity demand justice so that they can fully join modern liberal society, cohesive ethnic groups resistant to liberal expressive individualism like Kurds or Hmong, persecuted religious minorities such as Copts, nonurban nonelites such as leaders in the 4-H, and the rural poor can expect little attention from today's campus liberals.[7]

As Wilson Carey McWilliams has noted,

Notably, the groups that [liberal reformers] recognize are all defined by biology. In liberal theory, where our "nature" means our bodies, these are "natural" groups opposed to "artificial" bonds like communities of work and culture. This does not mean that liberalism values these "natural" groups. Quite the contrary: since liberal political society reflects the effort to overcome or master nature, liberalism argues that "merely natural" differences ought not to be held against us. We ought not to be held back by qualities we did not choose and that do not reflect our individual efforts and abilities. [Reformers] recognize women, racial minorities, and the young only in order to free individuals from "suspect classifications."

Class and culture are different. People are part of ethnic communities or the working class because they chose not to pursue individual success and assimilation into the dominant, middle-class culture, or because they were unable to succeed. Liberal theory values individuals who go their own way, and by the same token, it esteems those who succeed in that quest more highly than individuals who do not. Ethnicity and class, consequently, are marks of shame in liberal theory, and whatever discrimination people suffer is, in some sense, their "own fault." We may feel compassion for the failures, but they have no just cause for equal representation, unlike individuals who suffer discrimination for "no fault of their own."[8]

Yet while contemporary emphases in the humanities are consistent with the aspiration for autonomy that underlies the modern scientific venture, this conformity has not lent the humanities much long-term viability. In the absence of strongly articulated grounds for studying the liberal arts, in distinction to the modern project of autonomy and mastery, students and administrators are voting with their feet and pocketbooks to support the areas that show more promise for mastering nature. It is a sign of the success of the vision of autonomy advanced by the main players in today's humanities that their disciplines are shrinking and even disappearing, while STEM and economic pursuits grow. In the absence of a persuasive counternarrative, students, parents, and administrators understand that the best route to achieving the liberal conception of freedom is not in the humanities but elsewhere.

Today the liberal arts have exceedingly few defenders. The children of the left cultural warriors of the 1980s are no longer concerned with a more representative and inclusive canon. They are more interested in advancing the cause of egalitarian autonomy, now arrayed against the older liberal norms of academic freedom and free speech in the name of what some call "academic justice" and greater campus representation. While a rallying point is the cry for greater diversity, the ongoing project of "diversification" in fact creates greater ideological homogeneity on nearly every campus. Under the guise of differences in race, an exploding number of genders, and a variety of sexual orientations, the only substantive worldview advanced is that of advanced liberalism: the ascent of the autonomous individual backed by the power and support of the state and its growing control over institutions, including schools and universities.

The children of the right's cultural warriors have also largely abandoned interest in the role of formative books as the central contribution for cultivating self-government. Instead, today's "conservatives" are more likely to dismiss the role of the liberal arts not only as a lost cause, but not even worth the fight anymore.[9] Instead, reflecting priorities of the modern marketplace, they are more inclined to call for greater emphasis on STEM and economic fields—those fields that have gained prominence because of the victory of ideas in many of the "Great Books" that successfully proposed that old books might no longer be studied. Conservative political leaders like Governor Scott Walker of Wisconsin or Senator Marco Rubio of Florida disdain the liberal arts for not leading to high-paying jobs—and find unexpected support from President Obama, who criticized art history on the same grounds.

LIBERAL ARTS AGAINST LIBERALISM?

Contemporary circumstances have only accelerated the demise of the liberal arts. In the absence of forceful articulations of the reason for their existence on today's campuses, a combination of demands for "usefulness" and "relevance," along with the reality of shrinking budgets, is going to make the humanities increasingly a smaller part of the university. They will persist in some form as a "boutique" showcase, an ornament that indicates respect for high learning, but the trajectory of the humanities continues to be toward a smaller role in the modern university.

While few of today's professors of the humanities are able to articulate grounds for protest, I would think the humanities of old would be able to muster a powerful argument against this tendency. Its warning would be simple, recalling its oldest lessons: at the end of the path of liberation lies enslavement. Such liberation from all obstacles is finally illusory, for two simple reasons: human appetite is insatiable and the world is limited. For both of these reasons, we cannot be truly free in the modern sense. We can never attain satiation, and will be eternally driven by our desires rather than satisfied by their attainment. And in our pursuit of the satisfaction of our limit-less desires, we will very quickly exhaust the planet. Our destiny, should we enter fully down this path toward our complete liberation, is one in which we will be more governed by necessity than ever before. We will be governed not by our own capacity for self-rule but rather by circumstance, particularly the circumstances resulting from scarcity, devastation, and chaos.

Our commitment to a future of liberation from nature and necessity is illusory—it is the faith-based philosophy of our time. Religion is often accused of being incapable of drawing the right conclusions from evidence, but it seems to me that we have in plain view the greatest leap of faith in our time—namely, the response of the leadership of our nation and our institutions of higher learning to this very economic crisis that otherwise is used to justify a further displacing of the liberal arts in the name of economic viability. The crisis was itself precipitated by inattentiveness to the lessons of the traditional liberal arts, which in turn is today invoked as reason for its further neglect. The economic crisis, as everyone now knows, was the result of the idea that one could consume without limits, that a new kind of economics, combined with a liberatory politics, now allowed us to live beyond our means. The wanting of something was warrant for the taking of the thing. Our appetite justified consumption. Our want was sufficient for our satiation. The result was not merely literal obesity but moral obesity—a lack of self-governance of our appetites ultimately forced us on a starvation diet.

At our institutions of higher learning, a multitude of panels and conferences were organized on the economic crisis, bemoaning such things as the absence of oversight, lax regulatory regime, failures of public and private entities to exercise diligence in dispensing credit or expanding complex financial products. Yet one searches in vain for a university president or college leader—especially at the elite echelon—acknowledging that there was deep culpability on the part of their own institutions for our failure and our students' as well. After all, it was the leading graduates of the elite institutions of the nation who occupied places of esteem in top financial and political institutions throughout the land who were responsible for precipitating the economic crisis. Graduates of elite institutions occupied places of power and influence in the national economic order. Leaders of such educational institutions readily take credit for Rhodes and Fulbright scholars. What of those graduates who helped foster an environment of avarice and schemes of the get-rich-quick? Are we so assured that they did not learn exceedingly well the lessons that they learned in college?

If a renaissance is to come, it must be from a reconstituted education in the liberal arts. While a great patchwork of liberal arts colleges remains, most liberal arts institutions have been deeply shaped by presuppositions of the "new science." Hiring and promotion are made increasingly in accordance with demands of research productivity. Increasingly faculty members have been overwhelmingly trained at leading research institutions at which priorities of that new science dominate—priorities that many professors have internalized, even if those priorities do not mesh well in the liberal arts settings they occupy. As a result, many of these institutions incoherently aspire to elite status by aping the research universities, with many even going so far as to change their names from "College" to "University."[10]

Yet their reconstitution is not wholly out of reach. As "palimpsests," the older traditions persist. When we think of "liberal arts" more concretely, we rightly picture a numerous variety of institutions, most (at least once) religiously affiliated and variously situated. Most were formed with some relationship to the communities in which they were formed—whether their religious traditions, attention to the sorts of career prospects that the local economy would sustain, close connection to the "elders" of the locality, or strong identification with place and the likelihood of a student body drawn from nearby. Most sought a liberal education *not* that fully liberated its students from place and the "ancestral" but that in fact educated them deeply in the tradition from which they came, deepening their knowledge of the sources of their beliefs, confirming—not confronting—their faith, and seeking to return them to the communities from which they were drawn, where it was expected they would contribute to its future well-being and continuity.

Above all, liberal education did not so much "liberate" students from the limits of their backgrounds as it reinforced a basic teaching embedded deeply within its own cultural tradition, namely an education in limits. Often this conception of limits—conceived most often as based in morality or virtue—was drawn from the religious traditions of the particular institution. Most classical liberal arts institutions founded within a religious tradition required not only knowledge of the great texts of the tradition—including and especially the Bible—but corresponding behavior that constituted a kind of "habituation" in the virtues learned in the classroom. Compulsory attendance at chapel or Mass, parietal rules, adult-supervised extracurricular activities, and required courses in moral philosophy (often taught by the president of the college) sought to integrate the humanistic and religious studies of the classroom with the daily lives of the students.

Based upon a classical or Christian understanding of liberty, this form of education was undertaken with an aim to pointing to our dependence—not our autonomy—and the need for self-governance. As the essayist and farmer Wendell Berry has written, awareness of fundamental constraints of human action and behavior

> is not the condemnation that it may seem. On the contrary, it returns us to our real condition and to our human heritage, from which our self-definition as limitless animals has for too long cut us off. Every cultural and religious tradition that I know about, while fully acknowledging our animal nature, defines us specifically as *humans*—that is, as animals (if that word still applies) capable of living within natural limits but also within cultural limits, self-imposed. As earthly creatures, we live, because we must, within natural limits, which we may describe by such names as "earth" or "ecosystem" or "watershed" or "place." But as humans we may elect to respond to this necessary placement by the self-restraints implied by neighborliness, stewardship, thrift, temperance, generosity, care, kindness, loyalty, and love.[11]

An education based in a set of cultural conditions takes its lead from nature and works alongside it, through such practices as agriculture, craftsmanship, worship, story, memory, and tradition. It does not, in the model of the new science, seek nature's dominion or capitulation. A fundamental responsibility of education, then, is the transmission of culture—not its rejection or transcendence. A proper regard for and transmission of culture seeks to prevent the willful and aggressive exploitation of nature and Gnostic condescension toward culture, just as it cautions against the sort of roving and placeless form of deracinated philosophy of the sort recommended by an education in "critical thinking" and implicitly commended by our encouragement of our students to define success only by achieving a condition of placeless itinerancy demanded by our global economic system.

Finally, understood as a training in limits and care for the world and particular places and people, a liberal education—properly understood—is not merely a form of liberation from "the ancestral" or nature but an education in the limits that each imposes upon us necessarily to live in ways that do not tempt us to Promethean forms of individual or generational self-aggrandizement or the abusive effort to liberate ourselves from the limits and sanctions of nature. Particularly in an age during which we are becoming all too familiar with the consequences of living solely in and for the present and disconnected from "ancestral" concerns for living within our means—whether financially or environmentally—we would be well served to move beyond the extreme presentism of the contemporary era. We should instead seek a reinvigoration of an idea of liberal education in which we understand liberty to be the condition in which we come to terms with, and accept, the limits and constraints that nature and culture rightfully exert. As commended by ancient and religious traditions alike, liberty is not liberation from constraint but rather our capacity to govern appetite and thus achieve a truer form of liberty—liberty from enslavement to our appetites and avoidance of depletion of the world. In short, needful is the rescue of liberal education from liberalism.

CHAPTER SIX

The New Aristocracy

WHILE both sides in our current anticulture wars advance the liberal project of statist and market deracination and liberationism, achieved through expansion of individual autonomy and the Baconian project of conquering nature, students are wholly shaped to be working pieces within this system of "liberation." Increasingly today's students enter college solely with an aim to its "practical" application, by which is meant its direct relevance to its economic and technical applications, wholly unaware that there is a more capacious way of understanding "practical" to include how one lives as a spouse, parent, neighbor, citizen, and human being.

A two-tier system has arisen in which elite students are culled from every corner of the globe so that they may prepare for lives of deracinated vagabondage, majoring only in what Wendell Berry calls "upward mobility." Elite universities engage in the educational equivalent of strip mining: identifying economically viable raw materials in every city, town, and hamlet, they strip off that valuable commodity, process it in a distant location, and render the products economically useful for productivity elsewhere. The places that supplied the raw materials are left much like depressed coal towns whose mineral wealth has been long since mined and exported. Such students embrace "identity" politics and "diversity" to serve their economic interests, perpetual "potentiality" and permanent placelessness. The identities and diversity thus secured are globally homogenous, the precondition for a fungible global elite who readily identify other members capable of living in a cultureless and placeless world defined above all by liberal norms of globalized indifference toward shared fates of actual neighbors and communities. This in turn induces the globalized irresponsibility that was reflected in the economic interactions that precipitated the 2008 economic crisis but which is assuaged by calls for "social justice," generally to be handled through the depersonalized levers of the state. One of the most powerful ways that liberalism advances is by implicitly encouraging globalized narcissism while perpetuating a pervasive belief in its own benevolence.

Those who remain in the hamlets, towns, and cities are generally condemned to straitened economic circumstances, destined for low-wage and stagnant service industry jobs and cut off from the top tier of analytic-conceptual work that is reserved for elite graduates. They are rooted in economically deprived regions or survive on the outskirts of concentrations of elites, where they will struggle with inflated real estate prices either by overpopulating subpar urban housing or by living at a great commuting distance from work and entertainment. They generally own extraordinary and growing levels of debt, mainly college loans and mortgage debt, though the insistent demand that they participate fully in the broader economy as consumers doubtless leads them to accumulate other excessive debts as well. While there is always the chance that one of their children might move up the economic ladder—particularly via an elite college—in the main, fairly static differentiation now persists between the classes.

The fact that there can be both upward and downward movement, however, and that competition has now been globalized, leads all classes to share a pervasive anxiety. Because social status is largely a function of position, income, and geographic location, it is always comparative and insecure. While advancing liberalism assures that individuals are more free than ever from accidents of birth, race, gender, and location, today's students are almost universally in the thrall of an economic zero-sum game. Accusations of careerism and a focus on résumé building are not the result of a failure of contemporary education but reflect the deepest lessons students have imbibed from the earliest age: that today's society produces economic winners and losers, and that one's educational credentials are almost the sole determinant of one's eventual status. Today's students, in bondage to what the ancients would have called "servile education," generally avoid a liberal education, having been discouraged from it by their parents and by society at large. Liberalism spells the demise of an education once thought fitting for free people.

A main lesson learned particularly at elite colleges is the set of cooperative skills needed to ensure competitive advantage over those who are not in the elite, while recognizing that even those cooperative relationships are conditioned by a competitive system. Friendships and even romantic relationships are like international alliances—understood to serve personal advantage. In his book *Coming Apart*, Charles Murray reports that while stable marriages are more likely to contribute to various measures of life success, those most likely to form stable lifelong marriages are those at the elite levels of the social ladder.[1] Those in the lower tiers, meanwhile, are experiencing catastrophic levels of familial and social breakdown, making it all but impossible for them or their children to move into the upper tier. Elites are studiously silent about the familial basis of their relative success. Marital stability is now a form of competitive advantage for the upper tier, an advantage amplified by the insistence that family formation is a matter of individual choice and even an obstacle to autonomy. Having shaped the family in the image of the Hobbesian state of nature, its adoption by the strong is now one more tool for advantage over the weak.

The educational system, transformed into a tool of liberalism, is also ultimately the systemic creation of a new aristocracy of the strong over the weak. Liberalism's denouement is a society of deep, pervasive stratification, a condition that liberals lament even as they contribute in manifold ways to its perpetuation—particularly through its educational institutions. Liberalism's success thus fosters the conditions of its failure: having claimed to bring about the downfall of aristocratic rule of the strong over the weak, it culminates in a new, more powerful, even more permanent aristocracy that fights ceaselessly to maintain the structures of liberal injustice.

CLASSICAL LIBERALISM: ROOTS OF NEW ARISTOCRACY

Liberalism was justified, and gained popular support, as the opponent of and alternative to the old aristocracy. It attacked inherited privilege, overturned prescribed economic roles, and abolished fixed social positions, arguing instead for openness based upon choice, talent, opportunity, and industry. The irony is the creation of a new aristocracy that has enjoyed inherited privileges, prescribed economic roles, and fixed social positions. Even as liberalism's architects were forthright about their ambition to displace the old aristocracy, they were not silent about their hopes of creating a new aristocracy. Widespread abhorrence of the old aristocracy blinded many who acquiesced in liberalism's ambitions, even as it positively appealed to those who believed they would join the new aristocracy. Liberalism begins as a version of the Rawlsian Original Position, offering a veil of ignorance beyond which it is promised that there will be certain winners and losers. Rather than encouraging the embrace of relative economic and social equality, as Rawls supposed, this scenario was embraced by those of liberal dispositions precisely because they anticipated being its winners. Those inclined to deracination, rootlessness, materialism, risk taking, dislocating social change, and inequality in effect assured their own success, even as they appealed to the system's likely losers by emphasizing the injustice of aristocratic orders.

John Locke made clear that the new political and economic system he proposed in his *Second Treatise of Government*, liberalism's foundational text, would result in a different ruling class. In one of its key chapters, "Of Property," he divided the world into two sorts of persons: the "industrious and the rational" and "the querulous and contentious." In the world of prehistory, he wrote, both kinds of characters might have existed in some number, but a subsistence economy marked above all by absence of private property made it impossible to tell them apart. In such a world, each person gathers only enough food and requirements for each passing day, and any differences of talent, ability, and promise are wholly unrealized. Locke offers the Indians in the Americas as an example of such a "pre-history": subsistence societies in which neither "industriousness and rationality" nor "querulousness and contentiousness" can become salient. In such a world, a potential Bill Gates or Steve Jobs is so busy hunting or fishing for each day's meal that his potential goes wholly unrealized.

Yet if it were really true that the world had yet to distinguish between the two kinds of characters, Locke could not have described their existence. The world he is addressing is not, in fact, the one in which neither type of personality has been made manifest; rather, he describes a world in which the wrong people rule—namely "the querulous and contentious." He writes that a caste of lazy, complacent rulers, whose position is inherited and who govern without competition or challenge, will above all manifest querulousness. He proposes to replace this group with another—those animated by "industriousness and rationality," whose distinctive character is disallowed from full realization by the monopoly on wealth and power held by the querulous aristocracy.

But why would the commoners, who hold no position of power or wealth under aristocratic orders, and whose prospects for ruling are no better under a new dispensation, support trading one ruler for another? Locke has essentially admitted that one aristocracy—whose rule is based upon inherited position and wealth—will be replaced by another: what Jefferson was to call a "natural aristocracy" whose position is based upon higher degrees of "rationality" and "industriousness" than those in the general population. The same arbitrariness that affords aristocrats position and status in an aristocratic society also applies to the unequal distribution of "rationality" and "industriousness." The criteria for the ruling class change, but their arbitrary distribution remains.

It is here that Locke invokes the example of the New World, arguing that a society ruled by the "industrious and rational" will increase the productivity and value of property and thereby increase the wealth of all:

> To which let me add, that he who appropriates land to himself by his labour, does not lessen, but increase the common stock of mankind: for the provisions serving to the support of human life, produced by one acre of inclosed and cultivated land, are (to speak much within compass) ten times more than those which are yielded by an acre of land of an equal richness lying waste in common. . . . [Thus] a king of a large and fruitful territory [in the Americas] feeds, lodges, and is clad worse than a day-labourer in England.[2]

With this passage, Locke admits that the new economic, social, and political arrangements will bring about pervasive inequality, but suggests that it is to be preferred to an inequality in which the "querulous and contentious" govern, since everyone will be in a better material position. Inequality can be made bearable by the increased wealth that will be enjoyed as well by lower-status citizens. But Locke also tells us that inequality under the new system has the potential for nearly limitless differentiation. A subsistence economy is noteworthy for almost complete material equality between ruler and ruled. The aristocratic order is marked by pervasive inequality of rank and status, but those differences are relatively immovable. The proposed liberal order, by contrast, is premised on an elastic and expansive condition of inequality based upon economic prosperity as the method of differentiation between the higher and lower orders. The means of assuaging indignities, slights, resentment, or anger at the widening gap between high and low, successful and ineffective, rulers and ruled, is the promise of ever-increasing material prosperity for every member of society.

This is liberalism's most fundamental wager: the replacement of one unequal and unjust system with another system enshrining inequality that would be achieved not by oppression and violence but with the population's full acquiescence, premised on the ongoing delivery of increasing material prosperity along with the theoretical possibility of class mobility.

Today's classical liberals continue to advance this settlement as not only acceptable but worthy of celebration. Centuries after Locke, John F. Kennedy summarized this wager with the promise that "a rising tide raises all boats"—echoed often by Ronald Reagan—suggesting that even the flimsiest and cheapest boat could benefit from tsunami-sized differences for those at the top and the bottom. A vital element of this prosperity was the aggressive conquest of nature, particularly the intensive extraction of every potentially useful resource as well as the invention of processes and methods that would increase immediate value, regardless of future costs and consequences. Locke's thesis was that ongoing and continuous growth of wealth and prosperity could function as a replacement for social cohesion and solidarity. As the libertarian Friedrich Hayek understood, a society that embraces "rapid economic advance" will necessarily encourage inequality: "Progress at such a fast rate cannot proceed on a uniform front but must take place in echelon fashion."[3] Echoing Locke, Hayek recognizes that a society that advances rapidly and generates significant economic inequality will necessarily rely upon rapid and even accelerating advances in order to assuage discontent: "The enjoyment of personal success will be given to large numbers only in a society that, as a whole, progresses fairly rapidly. In a stationary society there will be about as many descending as there will be those rising. In order that the great majority should in their individual lives participate in the advance, it is necessary that it proceed at considerable speed."[4]

Hayek acknowledges that the liberal society will generate as much inequality as the order it replaced, or even more, but the promise of constant change and progress will ensure that everyone supports the liberal system. He is confident that even potentially titanic inequality—far outstripping the differences between peasant and king—will nevertheless lead to nearly universal endorsement of such a political and economic system.

There are now growing doubts over whether the promise of growth can be perpetuated. Humanity has confronted both the limits imposed by nature, as the costs of two centuries' economic growth become increasingly evident in today's accelerating climate change, and the decreasing likelihood that market capitalism will generate increasing prosperity for every part of society. Recent years have proven the foresight of Kurt Vonnegut's first novel, *Player Piano*, that an iron logic within market capitalism—namely the perpetual effort to suppress wages either by finding new low-wage markets or replacing humans with machines or computers—will increasingly reduce all but a few forms of work to drudgery and indignity. This recognition has led to a return of Locke's basic wager that a system that provided material comfort, no matter the vastness of inequality and absent likely prospects of growth and mobility between classes, would nevertheless satisfy most members of society. The most recent muse of Lockean liberalism is the economist Tyler Cowen, whose book *Average Is Over* echoes the basic contours of Locke's argument. While noting that liberalism and market capitalism perpetuate titanic and permanent forms of inequality that might have made dukes and earls of old blush, Cowen argues that we are at the end of a unique period in American history, a time of widespread belief in relative equality and shared civic fate, and entering an age in which we will effectively see the creation of two separate nations. Yet in his concluding chapter, fittingly entitled "A New Social Contract?," Cowen nevertheless concludes that liberalism will continue to enjoy widespread support:

> We will move from a society based on the pretense that everyone is given an okay standard of living to a society in which people are expected to fend for themselves much

more than they do now. I imagine a world where, say, 10 to 15 percent of the citizenry is extremely wealthy and has fantastically comfortable and stimulating lives, the equivalent of current-day millionaires, albeit with better health care. . . .

This framing of income inequality in meritocratic terms will prove self-reinforcing. Worthy individuals will in fact rise from poverty on a regular basis, and that will make it easier to ignore those who are left behind.[5]

Cowen predicts that this low-wage majority will settle in places that look a lot like Texas: cheap housing, some job creation, and subpar government services. Political leaders, he suggests, should consider erecting entire cityscapes of *favelas* with low rent and free internet, thus offering a virtual world of distraction from the grim poverty and spiritual desiccation that will become a permanent way of life for most citizens. Far from predicting that this dystopia will bring the end of liberalism and precipitate revolution against a social and economic system that re-creates the conditions of the old aristocracy that liberalism was supposed to overthrow, Cowen ends his book on this hopeful note: "We might even look ahead to a time when the cheap or free fun is so plentiful that it will feel a bit like Karl Marx's communist utopia, albeit brought on by capitalism. That is the real light at the end of the tunnel."[6]

RULE OF THE STRONG

Early-modern liberalism envisioned the autonomous individual giving rise to a system that resulted in radically different material attainments. As James Madison said of the world's first liberal order, the "first object of government" is protection of the "diversity in the faculties of men." Madison states in *Federalist* 10 that "from the protection of different and unequal faculties of acquiring property, the possession of different degrees and kinds of property immediately results." The first object of the government enshrined in our constitutional order is the protection of "diversity," primarily distinctions that are manifest in different economic attainments, but further, whatever differences arise from our "diversity of faculties." Liberal politics was conceived as a defense of those inequalities. Liberalism's second wave—Progressivism— argued that the rampant inequality that first-wave liberalism so successfully advanced was, in fact, an obstacle to the realization of true selfhood. Later liberals agreed that the first wave of liberalism had successfully undermined the old aristocratic political and economic forms, but concluded that its very successes had generated new pathologies that needed a reinvented liberalism. Liberalism today is widely identified as the opposite of early-modern liberalism's encouragement of economic liberty and hence stratification, instead stressing the imperative for greater economic equality.

But this embrace of economic equality was not intended to secure an opposite outcome to classical liberalism: rather, it sought to extend the weakening of social forms and cultural traditions already advanced by classical liberalism, with an end to increasing political consolidation. Under classical liberalism, this end could best be achieved by limiting government's authority over individuals. For progressive liberalism, it was best achieved by empowering the State to equalize the fruits of an increasingly prosperous society while intervening more actively in the realms of church, family, and even human sexuality.

Still, like its classical liberal forebear, progressive liberalism enlisted the support of the masses it would harm by emphasizing how it would correct the current system's injustices—in this case, the economic disparities generated by market capitalism. Yet the appeal to economic justice and taming of the market—never realized, of course—was advanced not ultimately in the name of greater equality but to secure the liberation of those living outside the guidelines and strictures of cultural norms by disassembling the social structures and cultural practices that supported the flourishing of the greater part of humanity. The progressive effort to make economic disparities more equal (without actually ever equalizing them) is driven by a deeper liberal imperative to equalize individuals' opportunity to be liberated from entanglements with others, particularly from the shared cultural norms, institutions, and associations that bind a people's fate together. Progressivism aims above all at the liberation of an elite whose ascent requires the disassembling of norms, intermediating institutions, and thick forms of community, a demolition that comes at the expense of these communities' settled forms of life. The deepest irony is that while our politics today is manifested as a clash of classical liberals against progressive liberals, we have seen a steady advance in both economic liberation and personal liberation. This is because progressive liberalism was never actually a foe of classical liberalism. Its true enemy was a kind of lived "Burkeanism": the way of life of much of humanity.

Nineteenth-century architects of progressive liberalism retained a main ambition of classical liberalism, namely the imperative to liberate individuals from any arbitrary and unchosen relationships and remake the world into one in which those especially disposed to expressive individualism would thrive. Few liberals were more forthright than John Stuart Mill in insisting that this liberation was essential to creating a new ruling class of wholly self-made individuals. In order to liberate these individuals from accident and circumstance, Mill insisted that the whole of society be remade for their benefit, namely by protecting their unique differences against oppressive social norms, particularly religious strictures and social norms governing behavior and comportment. Put another way, Mill argued that "custom" must be overthrown so that those who seek to live according to personal choices in the absence of such norms are at greatest liberty to do so.

In contrast to the argument by Yuval Levin that "the Great Debate" was between Burke and Paine, the "culture wars" of our time have more to do with differences between intuitive Burkeans and forthright disciples of Mill. This may surprise some, since Mill is sometimes taken to be a friend to conservatism, particularly libertarians. But he was no conservative: he was the midwife of modern liberalism, particularly through the arguments advanced in his classic 1859 work, *On Liberty*. Many of his libertarian admirers tend to assume that Mill's "Harm Principle" speaks primarily about limiting government's rule over individual liberty, but Mill was mainly concerned about the constraints that public opinion could forge. He opens the book by noting that in the England of his day, "the yoke of opinion is perhaps heavier, [and] that of law lighter, than in most other countries of Europe; and there is considerable jealousy of direct interference, by the legislative or executive power, with private conduct."⁷ Writing at the dawn of the era of popular sovereignty, he acknowledged that public opinion might someday be translated directly into popularly mandated coercive government power; but at that moment, "the majority have not learnt to feel the power of the government [as] their power, or its opinions their opinions." What concerned him was not coercive law but oppressive public opinion.

Forms of oppressive "opinion" were mainly manifest in everyday morality—what Mill witheringly criticized as "Custom." While Mill at times argued that a good society needed a balance of "Progress" and "Custom," in the main, he saw custom as the enemy of human liberty, and progress as a basic aim of modern society. To follow custom was to be fundamentally unreflective and mentally stagnant. "The human faculties of perception, judgement, discriminative feeling, mental activity, and even moral preference, are exercised only in making a choice. He who does anything because it is a custom, makes no choice."⁸

Custom may have once served a purpose, Mill acknowledges—in an earlier age, when "men of strong bodies or minds" might flout "the social principle," it was necessary for "law and discipline, like the Popes struggling against the Emperors, [to] assert a power over the whole man, claiming to control all his life in order to control his character."⁹ But custom had come to dominate too extensively; and that "which threatens human nature is not the excess, but the deficiency, of personal impulses and preferences."¹⁰ The unleashing of spontaneous, creative, unpredictable, unconventional, often offensive forms of individuality was Mill's goal. Extraordinary individuals—the most educated, the most creative, the most adventurous, even the most powerful—freed from the rule of Custom, might transform society. "Persons of genius," Mill acknowledges, "are always likely to be a small minority"; yet such people, who are "more individual than any other people," less capable of "fitting themselves, without hurtful compression, into any of the small number of moulds which society provides," require "an atmosphere of freedom."[11] Society must be remade for the benefit of this small, but in Mill's view vital, number. A society based on custom constrained individuality, and those who craved most to be liberated from its shackles were not "ordinary" people but people who thrived on breaking out of the customs that otherwise governed society. Mill called for a society premised around "experiments in living": society as test tube for the sake of geniuses who are "more individual."

We live today in the world Mill proposed. Everywhere, at every moment, we are to engage in experiments in living. Custom has been routed: much of what today passes for culture—with or without the adjective "popular"—consists of mocking sarcasm and irony. Late night television is the special sanctuary of this liturgy. Society has been transformed along Millian lines in which especially those regarded as judgmental are to be special objects of scorn, in the name of nonjudgmentalism.

Mill understood better than contemporary Millians that this would require the "best" to dominate the "ordinary." The rejection of custom demanded that society's most "advanced" elements have greater political representation. For Mill, this would be achieved through an unequal distribution of voting rights: those with a higher education would be accorded more votes. In less advanced societies, Mill argued, outright en-slavement of backward populations might be necessary until they could be sufficiently set on a path of progressive ad-vancement. This would mean, first and foremost, forcing them to work and care more about economic productivity than about wasteful activities like worship or leisure.

Americans, for much of their history, were not philosoph-ically interested in Burke but were Burkeans in practice. Most lived in accordance with custom—with basic moral assump-tions concerning the fundamental norms that accompanied a good life. You should respect authority, beginning with your parents. You should display modest and courteous comport-ment. You should avoid displays of lewdness or titillation. You should engage in sexual activity only when married. Once married, you should stay married. You should have children—generally, lots of them. You should live within your means. You should thank and worship the Lord. You should pay respect to the elderly and remember and acknowledge your debts to the dead.

Mill dismissed these behaviors as unthinking custom; Burke praised them as essential forms of "prejudice." In his *Reflections on the Revolution in France,* Burke wrote:

> In this enlightened age I am bold enough to confess that we are generally men of untaught feelings, [and] that, instead of throwing away our old prejudices, we cherish them. . . . We are afraid to put men to live and trade each on his own private stock of reason, because we suspect that this stock of each man is small, and that the individuals do better to avail themselves of the general bank and capital of nations and of ages. . . . Prejudice renders a man's virtue his habit, and not a series of

unconnected acts. Through just prejudice, his duty becomes part of his nature.[12]

Mill feared the tyranny of public opinion, expressed through custom, but Burke argued that the tyrannical impulse was far more likely found among the "innovators" and might be restrained by prejudice. It was the unshackled powerful who were to be feared, not the custom-following ordinary citizens. Burke saw a close relationship between the revolutionary and tyrannical impulse, made particularly insidious when the Great could claim the mantle of popular legitimacy: "The spirit of innovation is generally the result of a selfish temper. . . . When they are not on their guard, [the democratists] treat the humbler part of the community with the greatest contempt, whilst at the same time, they pretend to make them the depositories of their power."[13]

Society today has been organized around the Millian principle that "everything is allowed," at least so long as it does not result in measurable (mainly physical) harm. It is a society organized for the benefit of the strong, as Mill recognized. By contrast, a Burkean society is organized for the benefit of the ordinary—the majority who benefit from societal norms that the strong and the ordinary alike are expected to follow. A society can be shaped for the benefit of most people by emphasizing mainly informal norms and customs that secure the path to flourishing for most human beings; or it can be shaped for the benefit of the extraordinary and powerful by liberating all from the constraint of custom. Our society was once shaped on the basis of the benefit for the many ordinary; today it is shaped largely for the benefit of the few strong.

The results of this civilizational transformation are everywhere we look. Our society is increasingly defined by economic winners and losers, with winners congregating in wealthy cities and surrounding counties, while losers largely remain in place—literally and figuratively—swamped by a global economy that rewards the highly educated cognitive elite while offering bread crumbs to those left in "flyover country." Trends observed decades ago by Robert Reich and Christopher Lasch, who decried "the secession of the successful" and the "revolt of the elite," are today institutionalized through family, neighborhood, and schools, and replicated by generational succession.[14] Children of the successful receive preparation for entry into the ruling class, while those who lack those attainments are much less capable of affording, and insufficiently knowledgeable about, the basic prerequisites needed to push their children into the upper echelon.

Charles Murray and Robert Putnam have ably documented the self-perpetuating class divide that permeates modern American society.[15] Murray has shown through two fictional towns—wealthy Belmont and down-at-the-heels Fishtown—that the wealthy and powerful today enjoy family and marital stability, relatively low rates of divorce and out-of-wedlock birth, and low incidences of drugs and criminality, while on all these measures, Fishtown is descending into social anarchy. Murray has argued that Belmont simply needs to practice what it preaches—extol the virtues of virtue, rather than Millian "experimentalism" and value relativism—in order to instruct the denizens of Fishtown in what's needed to achieve success. Putnam has urged greater government support for citizens who are being left behind economically, proposing a host of programs to help them break the chain of social decay.

Both ignore what empirical observation should suggest: this condition is not an aberration from healthy liberalism but its fulfillment. From the outset, liberalism held forth the promise of a new aristocracy composed of those who would flourish with the liberation of the individual from history, tradition, nature, and culture, and the demolition or attrition of institutional supports that were redefined as limits or obstacles to liberty. Those who are best provisioned by disposition (nature), upbringing (nurture), and happenstance to succeed in a world shorn of those institutional supports aspire to autonomy. Even as the liberal family is reconstituted to serve as the launching pad for the autonomous individual, a landscape shorn of widespread social networks leaves those without advantages to succeed in liberal society among the underclass. Compounding their disadvantage is the "secession of the successful," the geographic withdrawal of a social and economic elite to a few concentrated areas, siphoning away those who might once have engaged in local philanthropy and the building of local civil society.

Murray believes that only willful denial born of progressive prejudice prevents the elite from extolling the virtues of stable family life and the personal qualities that help them maintain their social status. His claim neglects a different cause: the liberalocracy recognizes that it maintains its position through the advantages of stable social institutions, which serve ironically as the launching pad for Millian individuals. Such individuals flourish in a world stripped of custom, and the kinds of institutions that transmitted cultural norms, habituated responsibility, and cultivated ordinary virtues. Once such institutions were extensively disassembled—initially leading to the instability of families regardless of social class—the family could be reassembled along liberal lines, now shorn of those social supports but undergirded by support systems that can be purchased: a new form of servant class such as nannies and gardeners, along with modern-day tutors (SAT prep courses) and wet nurses (day care). The reconstructed family thus becomes one of the primary means by which the liberalocracy perpetuates itself, much as the aristocratic family was the source of wealth and status in earlier ages. Where the aristocratic family's status was bound up in the land and estate—hence emphasized generational continuity and primogeniture—the liberalocratic family rests upon loose generational ties, portable credentials, the inheritance of fungible wealth, and the promise of mobility. Meanwhile, the liberalocracy is studiously silent about the decimation of family and attendant social norms among what Locke might have called "the querulous and contentious," since the liberated individual who is the fruit of liberalism dictates that these people, now relegated to the underclass, must bear the cost of disassembling the social forms and institutions that traditionally supported families even among the disadvantaged.

In effect, liberalism advances most effectively through both classical and progressive liberalisms, the economic liberalism of Locke and the lifestyle liberalism of Mill, even while the two claim to be locked in battle. The destruction of social norms, culture, and the social ecology of supporting institutions and associations is advanced by both the market and the state. Advocates of the former (such as Murray) claim that the resulting deep inequality can be assuaged by moral admonition, while proponents of the latter (such as Putnam) argue that government can substitute for civil society and reconstruct the family that the liberalocracy has eviscerated. Both sides regard generational inequality as an aberration, rather than recognizing it as a key achievement of the liberal order.

The liberalocracy's self-deception is, in the main, neither malicious nor devious. Liberalism is arguably the first regime to put into effect a version of the "Noble Lie" proposed by Plato in the *Republic*, which claimed not only that the ruled would be told a tale about the nature of the regime, but more important, that the ruling class would believe it as well. The "noble lie" proposes a story by which the denizens of the "ideal regime" proposed by Socrates at once believe in their fundamental equality as members of a common family and in the natural basis of their inequality. While Plato proposed the "ideal regime" as a philosophic exercise, liberalism adopted a version of "the noble lie" in order to advance a similarly constituted order, in which people would be led to believe in the legitimacy of inequality backstopped by a myth of fundamental equality. Not only would day laborers be encouraged to believe that their lot in life would continuously improve by their ascent in the advance of the liberal order, but more important, the liberalocrats would be educated in a deep self-deception that they were not a new aristocracy but the very opposite of an aristocratic order. A primary vehicle has been a veneer of social justice and concern for the disadvantaged that is keenly encouraged among liberalocrats from a young age, often at the very educational institutions most responsible for their elevation into the elite. It is often these very same people who, upon encountering the discussion of the "Noble Lie" in the *Republic*, will pronounce their disgust at such subterfuge, all the while wholly unaware that the Cave they occupy has been rendered invisible by the artificial lighting designed to hide its walls.

CHAPTER SEVEN

The Degradation of Citizenship

HE term "liberal democracy" is widely used to describe the regime that today is regarded by most in the West as the sole legitimate form of political organization. "Liberalism" thus adjectivally coexists with the noun "democracy," apparently giving pride of place to the more ancient regime form in which the people rule. However, the oft-used phrase achieves something rather different from its apparent meaning: the adjective not only modifies "democracy" but proposes a redefinition of the ancient regime into its effective opposite, to one in which the people do not rule but are instead satisfied with the material and martial benefits of living in a liberal *res idiotica*. At the same time, the word "democracy" affords legitimation to the liberal regime from a populace whose purported consent stands in for a more robust form of citizenship. A degraded form of citizenship arises from liberalism's relentless emphasis upon private over public things, self-interest over civic spirit, and aggregation of individual opinion over common good.

We live in an age in which the ancient suspicion of democracy as a debased and corrupt form of government has been largely forgotten, or when encountered, is regarded as backward, authoritarian, and inhuman. The genius of liberalism was to claim legitimacy on the basis of consent and arrange periodic managed elections, while instituting structures that would dissipate democratic energies, encourage the creation of a fractured and fragmented public, and ensure government by select elite actors. If this were all that liberalism achieved, however, its patina of legitimation would quickly wear thin as a frustrated populace witnessed a growing divide between the claims of democracy and the absence of popular control. Instead, the true genius of liberalism was subtly but persistently to shape and educate the citizenry to equate "democracy" with the ideal of self-made and self-making individuals—expressive individualism—while accepting the patina of political democracy shrouding a powerful and distant government whose deeper legitimacy arises from enlarging the opportunities and experience of expressive individualism. As long as liberal democracy expands "the empire of liberty," mainly in the form of expansive rights, power, and wealth, the actual absence of active democratic self-rule is not only an acceptable but a desired end. Thus liberalism abandons the pervasive challenge of democracy as a regime requiring the cultivation of disciplined self-rule in favor of viewing the government as a separate if beneficent entity that supports limitless provision of material goods and untrammeled expansion of private identity.

ANTIDEMOCRATIC LIBERALISM

Liberalism's defenders are wont to note the dangers of democracy, particularly the threat of unconstrained majorities over the liberties of minorities. Prominent political observers such as Fareed Zakaria have noted the rise of "illiberal democracy" as a main threat to political stability, rights, and liberal political economy.[1] In the wake of the rise of nationalist populist movements such as those throughout Europe that oppose fundamental tenets of the European Union—particularly focused on the effectual elimination of national boundaries—and in the wake of Great Britain's "Brexit" vote and the election of Donald J. Trump to the U.S. presidency, political theorist and *Wall Street Journal* columnist William Galston devoted a column warning that "the most urgent threat to liberal democracy is not autocracy; it is illiberal democracy."[2] In the eyes of leading commentators, democracy remains as threatening and unsavory a regime as it did for Plato and Aristotle. While the ancient philosophers typically relegated democracy to the category of "vicious" or "debased" regimes, today's leading thinkers retain a notional allegiance to democracy only by constraining it within the strictures of liberalism, arguing that liberalism limits the power of the majority and protects freedoms of speech and the press, constitutional checks upon government. They also generally tend to favor fairly open markets and porous national borders, arguing that these arrangements secure prosperity for the nation's consumers while allowing globalized opportunities of economic mobility and opportunity.

Democracy is thus an acceptable legitimating tool only as long as its practices exist within, and are broadly supportive of, liberal assumptions. When democratic majorities reject aspects of liberalism—as electorates throughout western Europe and America have done in recent years—a growing chorus of leading voices denounce democracy and the unwisdom of the masses. American elites have periodically assayed the possibility of severely limiting democracy, believing that democracy will undermine policies preferred by experts. In particular, those favoring the expansion of liberalism beyond the nation-state, and thus policies that increase economic integration and the effective erasure of borders, have increasingly become proponents of further constraining democracy. One such authority is Jason Brennan of Georgetown University, who has argued in a book entitled *Against Democracy* that voters are consistently ill-informed and even ignorant, and that democratic government thus will ultimately reflect the deficiencies of the electorate.[3] Other libertarian-leaning liberals such as Bryan Caplan, Jeffrey Friedman, and Damon Root believe that when democracy threatens the substantive commitments of liberalism—which they maintain will be unavoidably the case, since uneducated and uninformed voters are illiberal—it might be better simply to consider ways to jettison democracy.[4] Brennan has instead called for rule by an "epistocracy," a governing elite with tested and proven knowledge to efficiently and effectively govern a modern liberal and capitalist state and social order.

The positions of these contemporary liberals are hardly new; they echo arguments made by other leading academics during the early part of the twentieth century, when there was growing confidence in the expertise of the administrative state and a dim view of the intellectual capacities of the electorate. In his 1973 book *The Crisis of Democratic Theory*, Edward A. Purcell masterfully documented the crisis of democratic theory that occurred as a result of early findings in the social sciences. A considerable quantity of early social-scientific data—including the first large-scale intelligence tests administered to a population that was seen as representative of, or even superior to, the average citizen, namely large numbers of troops during World War I—revealed consistently low I.Q. scores among broad swaths of the American populace. A steady stream of similar evidence led a great many leading social scientists of the 1920s and 1930s to call for a wholesale change in government.[5]

No less a figure than the 1934 president of the American Political Science Association—Walter J. Shepard—called for a fundamental reconsideration of America's traditional "faith" in democracy. The best evidence showed that the people were guided not by knowledge and wisdom but by ignorance and whim: "Not the reason alone, but sentiment, caprice, and passion are large elements in the composition of public opinion. . . . We no longer believe that the 'voice of the people is the voice of God.'"[6] Concluding that democracy was indefensible—for reasons similar to those suggested by Brennan, Caplan, Friedman, and others—Shepard urged his fellow political scientists to disabuse themselves of their unjustified faith in the public: the electorate "must lose the halo which has surrounded it. . . . The dogma of universal suffrage must give way to a system of educational and other tests which will exclude the ignorant, the uninformed, and the anti-social elements which hitherto have so frequently controlled elections."[7] Even John Dewey, who had once declared his own "democratic faith," in a long debate with Walter Lippmann acknowledged that the public was unlikely to be able to rise to the level of civic knowledge and competence demanded in a period of ever more complexity, and suggested that Whitman-like poets would be needed to provide a suitable and accessible "presentation" of the complex political and scientific information needed by the citizenry of a complex modern society.[8]

Concern over "democratic competence" of ordinary citizens has given rise not only to explicit critiques of democracy but to efforts to constrain democratic rule even by those who otherwise claim the democratic mantle. By one measure, progressive liberals appear strenuously to endorse democracy, and have been responsible for introducing many measures that increase more direct forms of democratic governance. Belief in greater direct popular control—evinced in such proposals as the initiative, recall, and referendum—were evidence of Progressive Era belief in the wisdom of the multitudes. Calls for education—with Dewey in the lead—were accompanied by claims that "the true Kingdom of God" was on the verge of realization.[9]

However, at the same time, a seemingly contradictory urge was evinced by many of the same progressives. Accompanying calls for *more* democracy were concomitant calls for *less* popular influence over policy making. Progressives were behind movements for more professionalization in government, above all civil service reform, with accompanying examinations and reduction in the numbers of political appointees within administrations (thereby severing the very electoral connection that progressives elsewhere sought to maximize). Progressives were the great proponents of a growth in government bureaucracy—the professionalization of politics—and the "science" of administration. Progressives were also in the vanguard of the promotion of the social sciences—including especially political science—as the best and most objective means of determining and implementing rational and objectively sound public policy in preference to the passing whims of the electorate. Major figures in the discipline like Woodrow Wilson sought to advance the scientific study of politics in the early years of the twentieth century, laying the groundwork for the rise of social scientific methodology as the necessary replacement of value-laden policy. Early figures in the institution of political science—such as Charles E. Merriam, Harold D. Lasswell, and George E. G. Catlin—called for the scientific study of politics as the prerequisite for objective public policy. "Nothing is more liable to lead astray," wrote A. Gordon Dewey of Columbia University, "than the injection of moral considerations into essentially non-moral, factual investigation."[10] Popular opinion was understood to give direction to those charged with policy creation. Democracy was thus limited to the expression of preferences, the collection of individual opinions that could then be collated and inform expert crafting of appropriate policy by expert administrators. Elton Mayo—a major social scientist in the 1920s—declared, "A world over, we are greatly in need of an administrative elite."[11] Armed with objective data from the social scientists, a credentialed, bureaucratic elite was expected to take cues from, and at times to lead and direct, irrational and ignorant democratic masses to accept objectively good public policy.

Consistent findings of civic ignorance and incompetence, indifference and misinformation are held by yesterday's and today's social scientists to be like the molecular makeup of water or laws of physics: measures of an objective and largely unalterable reality. Ironically, in an age in which science is interested in the ways that human activity is altering some basic assumptions about the natural world—especially climate change—a basic assumption of social science is that measurements of political "competence" are reflections of given facts. A deeper commitment to liberal ends renders such social scientists insensate to the ways that liberalism itself has fostered just such a "citizenry," that its main aim was to shape a liberal populace shaped primarily by individual interest and commitments to private ends. Whether social scientists conclude from measurements of civic ignorance and indifference that democracy should be jettisoned or that efforts at "civic education" should be increased, the basic assumption is the same: liberalism can correct what most contemporary liberals can't recognize that liberalism itself created. The ignorance of its own history and aims—the "presentism" of liberals—is one of liberalism's greatest defenses against recognition that it generates a civic catastrophe that it then claims it must cure by the application of more liberalism.

The persistent absence of civic literacy, voting, and public spiritedness is not an accidental ill that liberalism can cure; it is the outcome of liberalism's unparalleled success. It is an aim that was built into the "operating system" of liberalism, and the findings of widespread civic indifference and political illiteracy of past and present social scientists are the expected consequences of a successful liberal order.

For all of the differences between the progressives and the Framers, there nevertheless exists this striking continuity, at base a shared commitment of their common liberalism: both classical and progressive liberals are dominated by thinkers who praise the rule of the electorate even as they seek to promote systemic governmental features that will minimize electoral influence in the name of good policy outcomes. Indeed, it is curious and perhaps erroneous to debate the "democratic competence" of the American public, given that the system of government explicitly designed by its Framers was *not* to be democratic. The authors and defenders of the Constitution argued on behalf of the basic law by explicitly rejecting the notion that the Constitution would result in a democracy. They sought to establish a republic, not a democracy. As Madison famously wrote in *Federalist* 10, "hence it is that democracies have ever been spectacles of turbulence and contention: have ever been found incompatible with personal security or the rights of property; and have in general been as short in their lives as they have been violent in their deaths. Theoretic politicians, who have patronized this species of government, have erroneously supposed that by reducing mankind to perfect equality in their political rights, they would at the same time be perfectly equalized and assimilated in their possessions, their opinions, and their passions."[12]

Madison argued in particular that the dangers of democracies—conceived as small-scale direct democracies (in his mind, roughly corresponding to the size of the smallest American states) with a high level of participation by the citizenry—could be avoided by two recourses: first, by "the representative principle" of the new science of politics; and second, by "extending the sphere," that is, creating a large-scale political entity that would minimize the possibilities for civic combination ("faction"), increase the numbers of interests, and discourage political trust and activity among the citizenry. Even while retaining an electoral connection that would lodge ultimate sovereignty in the people, Madison was clear that representatives should not be excessively guided by the will of the people: the desired effect of representation, he argued, is "to refine and enlarge the public views by passing them through the medium of a chosen body of citizens, whose *wisdom may best discern the true interest* of their country."[13]

The best interest of the nation, according to James Madison in *Federalist* 10, was defense of "the first object of government," which was protection of "diversity in the faculties of men." The public realm existed for the sake of differentiation of the individual from others. In Madison's eighteenth-century view, government existed to "protect" individual pursuits and the outcomes of those pursuits, particularly as those individual differences would be manifest in unequal and varied attainments of property. Government exists to protect the greatest possible sphere of individual liberty, and does so by encouraging the pursuit of self-interest among both the citizenry and public servants. That "ambition must be made to counteract ambition" is conceived as the way by which separated and divided powers will prevent any particular person from centralizing and seizing power; but at the same time, the government itself is to be given substantial new powers to act directly on individuals in order at once to liberate them from the constraints of their particular localities, as well as to promote especially expansion of commerce as well as the "useful arts and sciences."

This political technology of liberalism aimed to liberate individuals from partial loyalties to particular people and places, and rather make us into individuals who, above all, would strive to achieve our own individual ambitions and desires. Part of the new technology of modern republicanism is what Madison called the "enlarged orbit," which not only would give rise to political leaders of "fit character" but would inculcate civic indifference and privatism among the citizenry. Madison hoped one consequence of enlarging the orbit would be heightened levels of mutual distrust among a citizenry inclined to advance particular interests, rendering them less likely to combine and communicate: "Where there is a consciousness of unjust or dishonorable purposes, communication is always checked by distrust in proportion to the number whose concurrence is necessary." A portrait arises of citizens who each face a large mass of fellow citizens whom they are inclined to mistrust, and a class of representatives who—while elected by the citizenry—take it upon themselves to govern on the basis of their views of the best interest of the nation.

It was Madison's hope that once the populace recognized its relative powerlessness in the public realm, the people would instead focus their attention on achievable private aims and ends. The political realm would attract the ambitious and those drawn to power, but would direct the growing power of the central government to increase individual prospects for the private ambitions of the individual, encouraging at the same time liberation from interpersonal ties and connections, fostering mistrust toward others so that interpersonal relations would be tenuous, fleeting, and fungible. One of the ways that it was hoped that modern republicanism would combat the ancient problem of political faction was not by commending public spiritedness but rather by fostering a "mistrust of motives" that would come about due to the large expanse of the republic, constantly changing political dynamics, the encouragement to "pluralism" and expansion of diversity as a default preference, and thus the shifting commitments of the citizenry. The ancient commendation of virtue and aspiration to the common good was to be replaced by the basic motivation of modern republicanism—the pursuit of self-interest that leads to the overall increase of power and thus fulfillment of desires.

The resulting liberal polity thus fosters a liberal society—one that commends self-interest, the unleashed ambition of individuals, an emphasis on private pursuits over a concern for public weal, and an acquired ability to maintain psychic distance from any other human, including to reconsider any relationships that constitute a fundamental limitation on our personal liberty. If Madison largely believed that this expression of individual differentiation would be manifest mainly through property, we can easily discern how this "external" form of differentiation was eventually "internalized" to forms of personal identity that would similarly require an active and expansive government to "protect the diverse faculties of men"—or whatever identity one might wish to assume. The idolization of "diversity" in the form of personal identity was sewn into the deepest fabric of the liberal project, and with it the diminution of a common civic and fostering of a common weal. The only common allegiance that would remain was to a political project that supported ever more individuation, fragmentation, and expansion of "diversity of faculties."

PUBLIC GREATNESS FOR PRIVATE ENDS

The very origins of mass democracy, then, appear to be bound up with efforts to minimize the creation of an engaged democratic citizenry. The dominant American political narrative—consistent from the time of the Founding to the Progressive Era and even to the present day—was simultaneously one that valorized democratic governance while devising structures that insulated government from excessive popular influence. More recent examples of the diminution of popular input and control over governance include the rise of "blue-ribbon commissions" and the growing influence of quasi-governmental but largely insulated agencies like the Federal Reserve.

Classical and progressive liberals shared not only the ambition of constraining democratic practice and active citizenship but a substantive vision of what constituted "good policy." Good policy for the Founders and progressives alike were those that promoted the economic and political strength of the American republic and the attendant expansion of power in its private and public forms. Liberalism sought not the taming and disciplining of power, along with the cultivation of attendant public and private virtues like frugality and temperance, but institutional forms of harnessing power toward the ends of national might, energy, and dynamism. As Publius—the pseudonym chosen by *Federalist* authors Madison, Alexander Hamilton, and John Jay—explains in defending the Constitution's bestowal of flexible powers upon the central government, unforeseeable future circumstances, particularly in the realm of foreign affairs, require the potential for the central government to wield incalculable, hence unlimited, power. "There ought to be a CAPACITY," writes Hamilton in *Federalist* 34, "to provide for future contingencies, as they may happen; and as these are illimitable in their nature, so it is impossible safely to limit that capacity. . . . Where can we stop, short of an indefinite power of providing for emergencies as they arise?"[14] It is, in fact, the very nature of the regime being planned—specifically, a commercial republic—that will prove an attraction for foreign ambitions, hence require the provision of "indefinite power": "If we mean to be a commercial people," continues Hamilton, "it must form a part of our policy, to be able one day to defend that commerce."[15] The argument echoes Machiavelli's: the Prince must have access to act with limitless power in defense of the State; the State's unleashed ambitions will lead to national wealth and greatness, making it more likely that other nations will seek to appropriate and invade; and thus, by a kind of iron syllogism, the ambition for national greatness and wealth makes the accumulation of unlimited power necessary and inescapable.

The Founders were aware that if their architecture was well designed, people's allegiance would shift from their natural affections for their local places and light instead on the power and magnificence of the capital. For this to occur, the intuitive understanding of liberty as the practice of self-government would need to be replaced by the experience of liberty as expanding "diversity of faculties"—whether unbounded increases in property and wealth or the experience of "more Being" that philosopher Richard Rorty described as the consequence of advancing liberal democracy. The Founders would not be surprised that a populace shaped by the modern form of private, material, individual, expressive liberty would displace allegiance to local and civic liberty, and that all attention and focus would be redirected to Washington, D.C., as the source and guarantor of expressive liberty.

This end would be advanced through an electoral arrangement that the Framers hoped would ensure the election to national office of men of particular distinction. The "enlarged orbit" of the nation and the prospects for greatness at the federal level would prove a draw to men of singular ambition whose interests aligned with the project of American national greatness. In an argument meant to dismiss fears of antifederalists that the central government would usurp the activities of the states, Hamilton actually confirmed that this was exactly the aim of the new federal government, thereby revealing the type of character that he believed would be drawn to the central government:

> I confess I am at a loss to discover what temptation the persons intrusted with the administration of the general government could ever feel to divest the States of the authorities of that description. The regulation of mere domestic police of a state appears to me to hold out slender allurements to ambition. Commerce, finance, negotiation, and war seem to compre-

hend the objects which have charms for minds governed by that passion: and all the powers necessary to those objects ought in the first instance to be lodged in the national depository. . . . It is therefore improbable that there should exist a disposition in the federal councils to usurp the [local] powers. . . . The possession of them . . . would contribute nothing to the dignity, to the importance, and to the splendor of the national government.[16]

Hamilton's argument points to an expected tendency in the new constitutional order, one promising, over time, that the role of the central government would be to increase the sphere of individual freedom through its particular auspices, and that the populace would eventually come to regard not only the central government as the protector of its freedoms but more direct and local forms of self-governance as obstacles to that freedom.

While many conservatives today claim that the Constitution sought to preserve a federalism that would ensure strong identification with more local identities, the underlying argument of *The Federalist* contradicts that claim. *The Federalist* lays out the conditions that would ensure that the populace would come eventually to identify more with the central than with the local and state governments. Both Madison and Hamilton acknowledge that humans naturally have greater affection for that which is in nearest proximity to themselves—albeit with an important caveat. Madison writes in *Federalist* 46 "that the first and most natural sentiment of the people will be to the governments of their respective states," while in *Federalist* 17 Hamilton writes, "It is a known fact in human nature, that its affections are commonly weak in proportion to the distance of diffusiveness of the object."[17] Both acknowledge that it is an abiding aspect of human nature to prefer what is close and more immediately "one's own" to that which is distant and less familiar.

To this forthright claim, however, each adds an important qualification. Hamilton goes on in *Federalist* 17 to reinforce this natural propensity to prefer what is near at hand, with an important exception: "Upon the same principle that a man is more attached to his family than to his neighborhood than to the community at large, the people of each state would be apt to feel a stronger bias towards their local governments, than towards the government of the union, *unless the force of that principle should be destroyed by a much better administration of the latter.*"[18] Madison echoes this stipulation in *Federalist* 46: "If, therefore, as has been remarked, the people should in the future become more partial to the federal than to the state governments, the change can only result from such manifest and irresistible proofs of better administration, as will overcome all their antecedent propensities."[19] Better "administration" will cause the natural fidelity to the close, the local, the familiar, to be "destroyed"; and by better administration, what is meant is governance by competent, enlightened, and effectual leaders who can effectuate the main commitments of the regime.

Unsurprisingly, Hamilton admits that this exception to the natural attraction of humans for the more local circumstance is likely to apply under the arrangements of the national system to be created by the Constitution. The concentration in the central government of men so disposed to regard as mere "slender allurements" the activities of the state governments is among the reasons that led Hamilton to conclude that it is to be expected that over time the federal government is likely to be better administered than those of the particular—that is, the state—governments. In *Federalist* 27 he includes the larger electoral districts and likelihood of attracting "select bodies of men" as among the "various reasons [that] have been suggested, in the course of these papers, to induce a probability, that *the general government will be better administered than the particular governments.*"[20] Reading this conclusion of *Federalist* 27 back into or forward to the caveat expressed in papers 17 and 46, we see that Publius clearly believes and intends that better administration at the federal level will lead to the displacement of local loyalties and engagement, and the redirection of attachments to the central government.

There can be little doubt who was right concerning where our attention would be focused: the authors of *The Federalist* understood that local devotions could ultimately be overcome by the power of the state to increase the "diversity of faculties," and to claim this definition of liberty as the only one worth possessing and pursuing. To be a democratic citizen entitled one to the expansion of individual ambitions and experiences, and one's civic duty was fulfilled by supporting a government that constantly advanced forms of expressive individualism. "Progressives" thus have had little success reining in the expansion of the private realm devoted to increasing acquisition of property and economic power. "Conservatives" have likewise had little success thwarting the expansion of individual expressivism, especially thwarting the advance of the sexual revolution. If anyone wants to know why the Republicans have failed to make the federal government smaller and to devolve power back to the states in significant ways (as they have claimed they seek to do at least since Goldwater, if not since FDR), we should recognize that such a reversal would go against the logic and the grain of the regime. It was designed so that power would accumulate at the center, and especially designed to attract to the center the most ambitious—those who will endeavor by dint of their constitutional ambitiousness to ensure that power continues to accumulate at the center. Commerce and war are the activities that most define the center, and those activities which accordingly have increasingly come to define the nation.

For all their differences, what is strikingly similar about the liberal thinkers of the Founding Era and leading thinkers of the Progressive Era were similar efforts to increase the "orbit" or scope of the national government concomitant with increases in the scale of the American economic order. Only in the backdrop of such assumptions about the basic aims of politics could there be any base presupposition in advance of the existence of "good policy"—and that policy tended to be whatever increased national wealth and power. In this sense—again, for all their differences—the Progressives were as much heirs as the Founders to the modern project of seeing politics as the means of mastering nature, expanding national power, and liberating the individual from interpersonal bonds and obligations, including those entailed by active democratic citizenship.

The Founders and the Progressives alike sought to increase the influence of the central government over disparate parts of the nation, while increasing economic efficiency and activity by means of investment in infrastructure and communication. Just as the Founders could promote the "useful arts and sciences" as one of the main positive injunctions of the Constitution, so the progressive John Dewey's praise of Francis Bacon as "the real founder of modern thought" would be frequently manifest in his praise of technological advance as tantamount to the advance of democracy itself.[21] For all of Dewey's valorization of "democracy," it should not be forgotten that his definition of democracy is bound up in whatever outcome would ultimately favor "growth." For the Founders and the Progressives alike, the expansion of what Madison described as "the empire of reason" should be paramount, and on that basis stated trust in popular government was to be tempered above all by fostering a *res idiotica*—a populace whose devotion to the Republic was premised upon its expansion of private ends and expressive individualism.

ILLIBERAL DEMOCRACY, RIGHTLY UNDERSTOOD

Writing of the township democracies he visited during his journey to America in the early 1830s, Alexis de Tocqueville expressed amazement over the intense commitment Americans exhibited toward their shared civic lives: "It is hard to explain the place filled by political concerns in the life of an American. To take a hand in the government of society and to talk about it is his most important business and, so to say, the only pleasure he knows."[22] Even as Tocqueville was to predict that the course of American democracy would lead to "individualism," isolation, and civic passivity, he observed in practice a phenomenon almost wholly its opposite: "[If] an American should be reduced to occupying himself with his own affairs, at that moment half his existence would be snatched from him; he would feel it as a vast void in his life and would become incredibly unhappy."[23]

Tocqueville observed practices of democratic citizenship that had developed antecedent to America's liberal founding. Its roots and origins, he argued, lie in the earlier Puritan roots of the American settlement, and in particular from the widely shared understanding of Christian liberty that he believed served as inspiration for the practices of democracy. Early in *Democracy in America*, Tocqueville describes "a beautiful definition of liberty" that he drew from Cotton Mather's *Magnalia Christi Americana*, or *The Ecclesiastical History of New-England*:

> Nor would I have you to mistake in the point of your own liberty. There is a liberty of corrupt nature, which is affected by men and beasts, to do what they list; and this liberty is inconsistent with *authority*, impatient of all restraint; by this liberty, *Sumus Omnes Deteriores* [we are all inferior]; 'tis the grand enemy of truth and peace, and all the ordinances of God are bent against it. But there is a civil, a moral, a federal liberty, which is the proper end and object of authority; it is a liberty for that only which is just and good, for this liberty you are to stand with the hazard of your own lives.[24]

Tocqueville here approvingly cites a distinction that can be traced to classical antiquity, between a liberty understood as license—"doing as one lists"—and liberty understood as the consequence of self-discipline, and in particular, free choice made on behalf of the good. Tocqueville commends a more contemporary articulation of a classical and Christian notion of liberty of doing what is consonant with the "just and the good," and not the liberal understanding that defines liberty as acting as one likes, so long as no one is physically harmed. This form of liberty, as the Mather citation suggests, is consistent with authority, authority that now seeks to order society so that citizens are encouraged to make only those decisions and undertake actions that are oriented toward the "just and good."

While liberals would come to see such authoritative ordering of society as the opposite of freedom—as "Puritanical"—Tocqueville on the contrary understood that the political translation of this form of liberty naturally entailed a certain kind of democratic practice. Democracy inspired by this "beautiful definition of liberty" demanded the discipline of self-rule, the especially challenging practice of political and personal self-limitation. Democracy required the abridgement of the desires and preferences of the individual, particularly in light of an awareness of a common good that could become discernible only through ongoing interactions with fellow citizens. Indeed, Tocqueville held that the very idea of the self as an "individual" was fundamentally transformed through such interactions: "Feelings and ideas are renewed, the heart enlarged, and the understanding developed only by the reciprocal action of men upon one another."[25]

For Tocqueville, such claims were more than merely theoretical: he believed that there was a straight line of influence from the Puritan understanding of liberty to the democratic practices of the townships of New England that he witnessed during his travels through the northeastern states. Observing the practice of self-rule—of a people imposing laws upon themselves directly—Tocqueville concluded that "the strength of free peoples resides in the local community. Local institutions are to liberty what primary schools are to science: they put it within the people's reach; they teach people to appreciate its peaceful enjoyment and accustom them to make use of it."[26] He stressed that it was the nearness and immediacy of the township that made its citizens more likely to care and take an active interest not only in their own fates but in the shared fates of their fellow citizens. By contrast, he noted a striking lack of attentiveness to more distant political centers of power, including both state and an even more distant federal government, where only a few ambitious men might govern but which otherwise was of little concern to the active citizens within the township. Tocqueville would have regarded a citizenry that was oblivious to local self-governance, but which instead directed all its attention and energy to the machinations of a distant national power, not as the culmination of democracy but as its betrayal.

Tocqueville argued that self-rule was the result of practice and habituation, and the absence of such self-rule would bring not the flourishing of freedom but reduction to servitude to distant rulers. Democracy, in his view, was defined not by rights to voting either exercised or eschewed but by the ongoing discussion and disputation and practices of self-rule in particular places with familiar people over a long period of time. Tocqueville did not regard such rule as utopic or without imperfections: "It is incontestable that people will often manage public affairs very badly, but their concern therewith is bound to extend their mental horizon and shake them out of the rut of ordinary routine." Democracy is not simply the expression of self-interest but the transformation of that what might have been narrow interest into a capacious concern for the common good. This can be effected only through the practice of citizens simultaneously ruling and being ruled by themselves: democracy "is not the laws' creation, but the people learn to achieve it by making the laws."[27]

Today's liberal critics of democracy—especially the emaciated forms of spectator politics that we call democracy—in effect condemn the deformed and truncated demotic actions of a degraded citizenry that liberalism itself has created. Leading liberals offer such degradation as evidence for the need to further sequester popular energies, offering instead the satisfactions of the private realm which will be further secured by the distant operation of elected plutocrats and bureaucratic functionaries of the liberal state.[28] Today's liberals who call for encouraging democratic participation through more extensive forms of civic education focused on national politics neglect the extent to which their cure is the source of the ills they would redress. It remains unthinkable that redress of civic indifference would require efforts to severely limit the power of the central state in favor of real opportunities for local self-rule. But those who readily display evidence of civic indifference or ignorance as evidence either for the need to limit or educate the citizenry unavoidably do so in the deeper commitment to strengthening the identification of politics with the actions of the liberal state, and by so doing, ensure the further degradation of citizenship.

We should finally not be surprised that even a degraded citizenry will throw off the enlightened shackles of a liberal order, particularly as the very successes of that order generate the pathologies of a citizenry that finds itself powerless before forces of government, economy, technology, and globalizing forces. Yet once degraded, such a citizenry would be unlikely to insist upon Tocquevillian self-command; its response would predictably take the form of inarticulate cries for a strongman to rein in the power of a distant and ungovernable state and market. Liberalism itself seems likely to generate demotic demands for an illiberal autocrat who promises to protect the people against the vagaries of liberalism itself. Liberals are right to fear this eventuality, but persist in willful obliviousness of their own complicity in the birth of the illiberal progeny of the liberal order itself.

Conclusion: Liberty after Liberalism

IBERALISM has failed because liberalism has succeeded. As it becomes fully itself, it generates endemic pathologies more rapidly and pervasively than it is able to produce Band-aids and veils to cover them. The result is the systemic rolling blackouts in electoral politics, governance, and economics, the loss of confidence and even belief in legitimacy among the citizenry, that accumulate not as separable and discrete problems to be solved within the liberal frame but as deeply interconnected crises of legitimacy and a portent of liberalism's end times.

The narrowing of our political horizons has rendered us incapable of considering that what we face today is not a set of discrete problems solvable by liberal tools but a systemic challenge arising from pervasive invisible ideology. The problem is not in just one program or application but in the operating system itself. It is almost impossible for us to conceive that we are in the midst of a legitimation crisis in which our deepest systemic assumptions are subject to dissolution.

The "Noble Lie" of liberalism is shattering because it continues to be believed and defended by those who benefit from it, while it is increasingly seen as a lie, and not an especially noble one, by the new servant class that liberalism has produced. Discontent is growing among those who are told by their leaders that their policies will benefit them, even as liberalism remains an article of ardent faith among those who ought to be best positioned to comprehend its true nature. But liberalism's apologists regard pervasive discontent, political dysfunction, economic inequality, civic disconnection, and populist rejection as accidental problems disconnected from systemic causes, because their self-deception is generated by enormous reservoirs of self-interest in the maintenance of the present system. This divide will only widen, the crises will become more pronounced, the political duct tape and economic spray paint will increasingly fail to keep the house standing. The end of liberalism is in sight.

This denouement might take one of two forms. In the first instance, one can envision the perpetuation of a political system called "liberalism" that, becoming fully itself, operates in forms opposite to its purported claims about liberty, equality, justice, and opportunity. Contemporary liberalism will increasingly resort to imposing the liberal order by fiat—especially in the form of the administrative state run by a small minority who increasingly disdain democracy. End runs around democratic and populist discontent have become the norm, and backstopping the liberal order is the ever more visible power of a massive "deep state," with extensive powers of surveillance, legal mandate, police power, and administrative control. These methods will continue to be deployed despite liberalism's claim to rest on consent and popular support. Such a conclusion is paradoxical, not unlike Tocqueville's conclusion in *Democracy in America*, in which he envisions democracy culminating in a new form of despotism.

But the instabilities that surely would accompany this outcome suggest a second possible denouement—the end of liberalism and its replacement by another regime. Most people envisioning such scenarios rightly warn of the likely viciousness of any successor regime, and close to hand are the examples of the collapse of the Weimar Republic and the rise of fascism, and Russia's brief flirtation with liberalism before the imposition of communism. While these brutal and failed examples suggest that such possibilities are unlikely to generate widespread enthusiasm even in a postliberal age, some form of populist nationalist authoritarianism or military autocracy seems altogether plausible as an answer to the anger and fear of a postliberal citizenry.

While growing discontent in Western liberal democracies suggests that either outcome is a realistic possibility, neither is to be wished for in the form it is likely to take. Yet the failure of liberalism itself invites this outcome, even as the unwillingness of liberalism's defenders to perceive their own complicity in fostering widespread discontent among their fellow citizens only makes such a lamentable outcome more likely. Liberalism's defenders today regard their discontented countrymen as backward and recidivist, often attributing to them the most vicious motivations: racism, narrow sectarianism, or bigotry, depending upon the issue at hand. To the extent that liberalism regards itself as a self-healing, perpetual political machine, it remains almost unthinkable for its apologists to grasp that its failure may lead to its replacement by a cruel and vicious successor. No serious effort to conceive a humane postliberal alternative is likely to emerge from the rear-guard defenders of a declining regime.

AFTER LIBERALISM

Imagining a humane alternative to either liberalocratic despotism or the rigid and potentially cruel authoritarian regime that may replace it seems at best a parlor game, at worst a fool's errand. Yet engaging in the activity once central to political philosophy—the negotiation between the utopian and realistic, begun by Plato in the *Republic*—remains essential if the grimmer scenarios of a life after liberalism are to be avoided, and something potentially better brought into being. If today only the barest outlines may be discerned amid a landscape so completely shaped by our liberal age, tentative first steps are required. The destination is unknown and unforeseeable, and the journey will probably require generations to complete.

I conclude by taking three of those initial steps.

- First, the achievements of liberalism must be acknowledged, and the desire to "return" to a preliberal age must be eschewed. We must build upon those achievements while abandoning the foundational reasons for its failures. There can be no going back, only forward.

- Second, we must outgrow the age of ideology. Of the three great modern ideologies, only the oldest and most resilient remains, but liberals mistook the fall of its competitors for the end of history rather than the pyrrhic victory it really was. The gap between liberalism's claims about itself and the lived reality of the citizenry widens to the point that the lie can no longer be accepted. Instead of trying to conceive a replacement ideology (or returning to some updated version of an alternative, such as a renascent Marxism), we should focus on developing practices that foster new forms of culture, household economics, and polis life.

- Third, from the cauldron of such experience and practice, a better theory of politics and society might ultimately emerge. Such a theory must eschew liberalism's ideological dimensions yet be cognizant of its achievements and the rightful demands it makes—particularly for justice and dignity. The outlines of such a theory are already discernible, guided by liberalism's own retention of essential concepts from a preliberal age— especially that of liberty—and reinforced by experience and practice essential for a humane life. This first step toward a new theory is the most tentative, but it faces in a confident direction, given the perpetual appeal of certain basic political ideals that have been present in the Western tradition since antiquity.

NO RETURN

Like all human projects, liberalism is not without its achievements. Living within its cave, liberal humanity has been too self-congratulatory about its successes; hence the need to show in these pages its deeper costs. But if we hope to create a humane postliberal future, we cannot pretend that the age of liberalism did not happen or that its basic contours can simply be jettisoned in some sort of restoration of an idyllic preliberal age. That age never existed—though, at the same time, the past can and ought to instruct as we move forward toward new possibilities. Any steps toward a postliberal age must begin with a sympathetic appreciation of liberalism's appeal and an effort to realize the admirable ideals that liberalism often only promised.

While liberalism pretended to be a wholly new edifice that rejected the political architecture of all previous ages, it naturally drew upon long developments from antiquity to the late Middle Ages. A significant part of its appeal was not that it was something wholly new but that it drew upon deep reservoirs of belief and commitment. Ancient political philosophy was especially devoted to the question of how best to avoid the rise of tyranny, and how best to achieve the conditions of political liberty and self-governance. The basic terms that inform our political tradition—liberty, equality, dignity, justice, constitutionalism—are of ancient pedigree. The advent of Christianity, and its development in the now largely neglected political philosophy of the Middle Ages, emphasized the dignity of the individual, the concept of the person, the existence of rights and corresponding duties, the paramount importance of civil society and a multiplicity of associations, and the concept of limited government as the best means of forestalling the inevitable human temptation toward tyranny. Liberalism's most basic appeal was not its rejection of the past but its reliance upon basic concepts that were foundational to the Western political identity.

The architects of liberalism embraced the language and terms of the classical and Christian traditions even as they transformed both meaning and practice. They especially rejected the classical and Christian understanding of human beings as fundamentally relational creatures—"social and political animals"—and proposed that liberty, rights, and justice could best be achieved by radically redefining human nature. The result was an advance in rendering the political longings of the intellectual West vastly more accessible and popular, but at the cost of establishing a political world that undermined those ideals. Liberalism's break with the past was founded on a false anthropology; yet at the same time, those ideals have been rendered more universal and secure in significant part through the growing discontent with liberalism's failure to realize them.

A vast disconnect once existed between the philosophy of the West and its practices. The ideals of liberty, equality, and justice coexisted with extensive practices of slavery, bondage, inequality, disregard for the contributions of women, and arbitrary forms of hierarchy and application of law. Liberalism was a sign of the profound success of the West's most fundamental philosophical commitments, a manifestation of a widespread demand that daily practices should more closely conform to ideals.

Yet while advancing these ideals, liberalism ultimately betrayed them through its disfiguring conception of human nature and the politics, economics, education, and application of technology that resulted from it. Today, as in past centuries, a vast disconnect exists between our stated ideals and our practices, but unlike past eras, the ideological nature of liberalism makes our current disconnection difficult to perceive, because now the failure to achieve those ideals is endemic to liberalism itself. The word "freedom" is embraced as the fundamental commitment of our age, but in vast swaths of life, freedom seems to recede—many citizens, for instance, believe they have little actual control over or voice in their government. Motivation by many voters in advanced democracies reflects not the confident belief that their voice is being heard, but the conviction that their vote is against a system that no longer recognizes the claim to self-rule. At the same time, freedom in areas such as consumer choice expands exponentially, leading many to take on too much debt to feed ultimately unfulfillable cravings. We effectively possess little self-government, either as citizens over our leaders or as individuals over our appetites. Citizens under liberalism are assured of our civic potency while experiencing political weakness and engaging in infinite acts of choice that are only deeper expressions of thralldom. We have endless choices of the kind of car to drive but few options over whether we will spend large parts of our lives in soul-deadening boredom within them. All the while, liberalism claims that we are free, and in spite of pervasive misgivings and growing discontent, we believe in an equivalence of word and deed.

Part of moving toward a postliberal age is recognizing that while liberalism's initial appeal was premised upon laudatory aspirations, its successes have often been based on a disfigurement of those aspirations. Its defenders often point to the liberation of women from conditions of inequality as a significant example of liberalism's success, and regard any critique of liberalism as a proposal to thrust women back into preliberal bondage. Yet the main practical achievement of this liberation of women has been to move many of them into the workforce of market capitalism, a condition that traditionalists like Wendell Berry as well as Marxist political theorists like Nancy Fraser regard as a highly dubious form of liberation.[1] All but forgotten are arguments, such as those made in the early Republic, that liberty consists of independence from the arbitrariness not only of a king but of an employer. Today we consider the paramount sign of the liberation of women to be their growing emancipation from their biology, which frees them to serve a different, disembodied body—"corporate" America—and participate in an economic order that effectively obviates any actual political liberty. Liberalism posits that freeing women from the household is tantamount to liberation, but it effectively puts women and men alike into a far more encompassing bondage.

Liberalism arose by appeal to an ennobling set of political ideals and yet realized new and comprehensive forms of degradation. Put less charitably, the architects of liberalism intentionally appropriated widely shared political ideals and subverted them to the advantage of those most capable of benefiting from new definitions of liberty, democracy, and republicanism.[2] Building on liberalism's successes means recognizing both the legitimacy of its initial appeal and the deeper reasons for its failure. It means offering actual human liberty in the form of both civic and individual self-rule, not the ersatz version that combines systemic powerlessness with the illusion of autonomy in the form of consumerist and sexual license. Liberalism was both a boon and a catastrophe for the ideals of the West, perhaps a necessary step whose failures, false promises, and unfulfilled longings will lead us to something better.

THE END OF IDEOLOGY

Liberalism was launched with the claim that it would "take men as they are," grounding a new politics upon a clear-sighted realism about human nature. Yet its claims about humans "as they are" were premised upon the fiction of radically autonomous humans in a State of Nature. The political, social, and economic order shaped around this disfigured view of human nature succeeded in remaking people in this image, but the project had the predictable effect of liberating them from the reality of relational life. Liberalism has always been animated by a vision of how humans "ought" to live, but it masked these normative commitments in the guise of neutrality. Like its competitor ideologies, it called forth a massive political and economic apparatus to fulfill its vision—in the process both reshaping and damaging humanity. A more humane politics must avoid the temptation to replace one ideology with another. Politics and human community must percolate from the bottom up, from experience and practice.

One of liberalism's most damaging fictions was the theory of consent, an imaginary scenario in which autonomous, rational calculators formed an abstract contract to establish a government whose sole purpose was to "secure rights." This view of consent relegated all "unchosen" forms of society and relationships to the category of "arbitrary" and thus suspect if not illegitimate. Liberalism today has successfully expanded itself from a political project to a social and even familial one, acting most often as solvent upon all social bonds. Yet as liberalism faces more challenging frontiers—especially those religious institutions that fundamentally reject liberal premises—we witness an increasingly visible and active government advancing its project through efforts to control religious and familial practice and belief.[3]

Liberalism takes the fundamental position that "consent" to any relationship or bond can be given only when people are completely and perfectly autonomous and individual. Only then are they able to consciously and purposefully engage in forms of utilitarian relationality, and also thereby capable of remaking such bonds when they prove to be unsatisfactory. I recall a chilling conversation when I was teaching at Princeton University about a book that had recently appeared about the Amish. We were discussing the practice of Rumspringa—literally, "running around"—a mandatory time of separation of young adults from the community during which they partake of the offerings of modern liberal society.[4] The period of separation lasts usually about a year, at the end of which the young person must choose between the two worlds. An overwhelming number, approaching 90 percent, choose to return to be baptized and to accept norms and strictures of their community that forbid further enjoyment of the pleasure of liberal society. Some of my former colleagues took this as a sign that these young people were in fact not "choosing" as free individuals. One said, "We will have to consider ways of freeing them." Perfect liberal consent requires perfectly liberated individuals, and the evidence that Amish youth were responding to the pull of family, community, and tradition marked them as unfree.

Liberalism renders such ties suspect while papering over the ways in which it has shaped its own youth to adopt a particular form of life, set of beliefs, and worldview; these are never subject to appraisal by any standards outside liberalism itself. The traditional culture of the Amish (one can also think of other examples) gives its young a choice about whether they will remain within that culture, but only one option is seen as an exercise of choice. Acquiescence to liberalism, however unreflective, is "tacit consent," yet membership in a traditional community is "oppression" or "false consciousness."

Under this double standard, religious, cultural, and familial membership is an accident of birth. Yet for modern humanity in the advanced West and increasingly the world, liberalism is equally an unwitting inheritance, and any alternatives are seen as deeply suspect and probably in need of liberal intervention. Liberalism further overlooks the way that culture itself is a deeper form of consent. Culture and tradition are the result of accumulations of practice and experience that generations have willingly accrued and passed along as a gift to future generations. This inheritance is the result of a deeper freedom, the freedom of intergenerational interactions with the world and one another. It is the consequence of collected practice, and succeeding generations may alter it if their experience and practices lead to different conclusions.

The sustenance of existing cultural and religious practices and the building of new communities will require far more conscientiousness than the passive acquiescence now fostered toward liberalism itself. It is an irony (and arguably a benefit of a liberal age) that today it is liberalism itself that silently shapes an unreflective population, and that the development of new cultures is what requires conscious effort, deliberation, reflectiveness, and consent. This is true especially for religious communities in an age in which liberalism has become increasingly hostile to self-imposed limitations and strictures that it finds abhorrent, particularly, but not only, in the domain of personal and sexual autonomy—a stance that many see as betrayal of liberalism rather than its culmination. But this very conflict, by showing the lengths to which liberalism will go to reshape the world in its own image, shows the need for alternative communities and new cultures that will live outside the gathering wreckage of liberalism's twilight years.

THE ADVENT OF POSTLIBERAL PRACTICE AND TOWARD A NEW BIRTH OF THEORY

Already there is evidence of growing hunger for an organic alternative to the cold, bureaucratic, and mechanized world liberalism offers. While especially evident in the remnants of orthodox religious traditions—not only in self-contained communities like the Amish but increasingly in growing international movements of Catholics, Protestants, Jews, and others—there is also growing interest in proposals for a "Benedict Option," most interestingly proposed and explored in the book of that name by Rod Dreher.[5] The building up of practices of care, patience, humility, reverence, respect, and modesty is also evident among people of no particular religious belief, homesteaders and "radical homemakers" who—like their religious counterparts—are seeking within households and local communities and marketplaces to rediscover old practices, and create new ones, that foster new forms of culture that liberalism otherwise seeks to eviscerate.[6]

Often called a counterculture, such efforts should better understand themselves as a counter-anticulture. Building a culture in the midst of today's anticulture is a profound challenge because of the flattened cultural wasteland produced by modern liberalism, as well as its jealous hostility to competitors. A culture is built from the bottom up, and like an organism, it maintains its DNA by passing itself on to subsequent generations. A self-conscious effort to build a new culture exists in basic contradiction to more organic origins and development of cultural practice. Yet the unique context of liberalism's blighted cultural landscape demands something new. Ironically, given the default choice-based philosophy that liberalism has bequeathed to us, what might someday become a nonvoluntarist cultural landscape must be born out of voluntarist intentions, plans, and actions.

Such efforts should focus on building practices that sustain culture within communities, the fostering of household economics, and "polis life," or forms of self-governance that arise from shared civic participation. All such practices arise from local settings that resist the abstraction and depersonalization of liberalism, and from which habits of memory and mutual obligation arise. While culture is cultivated and passed on in the most immediate way in households, it is developed

in and through a community of families and centers especially on rituals surrounding birth, coming of age, marriage, and
death. Culture takes into account local circumstances, often
drawing sustenance and inspiration from facts of local geog-
raphy and history. It passes memory down through generations via story and song, not the sort packaged in Hollywood
or on Madison Avenue, but arising from voices in particular
places. And as the word suggests, it is nearly always linked to
"cult," understanding the local to be bound to and ultimately
an expression of the universal and eternal, the divine and
sublime. Such practices give rise to the only real form of diversity, a variety of cultures that is multiple yet grounded in
human truths that are transcultural and hence capable of
being celebrated by many peoples.

A counter-anticulture also requires developing economic
practices centered on "household economics," namely, economic habits that are developed to support the flourishing of
households but which in turn seek to transform the household into a small economy. Utility and ease must be rejected
in preference to practices of local knowledge and virtuosity.
The ability to do and make things for oneself—to provision
one's own household through the work of one's own and one's
children's hands—should be prized above consumption and
waste. The skills of building, fixing, cooking, planting, pre-
serving, and composting not only undergird the independence and integrity of the home but develop practices and
skills that are the basic sources of culture and a shared civic
life. They teach each generation the demands, gifts, and
limits of nature; human participation in and celebration of
natural rhythms and patterns; and independence from the

culture-destroying ignorance and laziness induced by the ersatz freedom of the modern market.

Along with the arts of household economics is the greater challenge of minimizing one's participation in the abstract and depersonalizing nature of the modern economy. The skills and dispositions gained in the household should be extended to an economy of households, in which friendships, places, and histories are relevant considerations in economic transactions. An economy that prizes facelessness fosters citizens who cannot see, hear, or speak properly about critical relationships to one another and to the world. Our economy encourages a pervasive ignorance about the sources and destinies of the goods we buy and use, and this ignorance in turn promotes indifference amid an orgy of consumption. Like liberal politics, the economy promotes a concern solely for the short term, hence narrows our temporal horizon to exclude knowledge of the past and concern for the future. Such an economy creates debtors who live for the present, confident that the future will take care of itself while consuming the goods of the earth today in ways that make it less likely that that future ever exists. Local markets, by contrast, foster relations built over time and in place, and necessarily point us beyond individual calculation. Sellers and buyers make their exchanges with an awareness of how their relationships help build a better community, aware that some profit will be reinvested at home for the benefit of friends, neighbors, and generations yet unborn.

A greater emphasis upon household economics and local exchange must be accompanied by greater political self-governance. Today we measure political health by the percentage of the voting-age population that actually votes, and while this percentage has grown in the past few elections, even this supposed sign of civic health hovers between 50 and 60 percent. Yet the national obsession with presidential electoral politics and the reduction of political conversation and debate to issues arising in the federal government are signs more of civic dis-ease than of health. Politics is reduced largely to a spectator sport, marketed and packaged as a distraction for a passive population. Elections provide the appearance of self-governance but mainly function to satiate any residual civic impulse before we return to our lives as employees and consumers.

When Tocqueville visited America in the late 1820s, he marveled at Americans' political do-it-yourself spirit. Unlike his fellow Frenchmen, who were passively acquiescent to a centralized aristocratic order, Americans would readily gather in local settings to solve problems. In the process they learned the "arts of association." They were largely indifferent to the distant central government, which then exercised relatively few powers. Local township government, Tocqueville wrote, was the "schoolhouse of democracy," and he praised the commitment of citizens to secure the goods of common life not only for the ends they achieved but for the habits and practices they fostered and the beneficial changes they wrought on citizens themselves. The greatest benefit of civic participation, he argued, was not its effects in the world, but those on the relations among people engaged in civic life: "Citizens who are bound to take part in public affairs must turn from the private interests and occasionally take a look at something other than themselves. As soon as common affairs are treated in common, each man notices that he is not as independent of his fellows as he used to suppose and that to get their help he must often offer his aid to them."[7]

For a time, such practices will be developed within intentional communities that will benefit from the openness of liberal society. They will be regarded as "options" within the liberal frame, and while suspect in the broader culture, largely permitted to exist so long as they are nonthreatening to the liberal order's main business. Yet it is likely from the lessons learned within these communities that a viable postliberal political theory will arise, one that begins with fundamentally different anthropological assumptions not arising from a supposed state of nature or concluding with a world-straddling state and market, but instead building on the fact of human relationality, sociability, and the learned ability to sacrifice one's narrow personal interest not to abstract humanity, but for the sake of other humans. With the demise of the liberal order, such countercultures will come to be seen not as "options" but as necessities.

Still, the impulse to devise a new and better political theory in the wake of liberalism's simultaneous triumph and demise is a temptation that must be resisted. The search for a comprehensive theory is what gave rise to liberalism and successor ideologies in the first place. Calls for restoration of culture and the liberal arts, restraints upon individualism and statism, and limits upon liberalism's technology will no doubt prompt suspicious questions. Demands will be made for comprehensive assurances that inequalities and injustices arising from racial, sexual, and ethnic prejudice be preemptively forestalled and that local autocracies or theocracies be legally prevented. Such demands have always contributed to the extension of liberal hegemony, accompanied by simultaneous self-congratulation that we are freer and more equal than ever, even as we are more subject to the expansion of both the state and market, and less in control of our fate.

By now we should entertain the possibility that liberalism continues to expand its global dominion by deepening inequality and constraining liberty in the name of securing their opposite. Perhaps there is another way, starting with the efforts of people of goodwill to form distinctive countercultural communities in ways distinct from the deracinated and depersonalized form of life that liberalism seems above all to foster. As the culmination of liberalism becomes more fully visible, as its endemic failures throw more people into economic, social, and familial instability and uncertainty, as the institutions of civil society are increasingly seen to have been hollowed out in the name of individual liberation, and as we discover that our state of ever-perfected liberty leaves us, as Tocqueville predicted, both "independent and weak," such communities of practice will increasingly be seen as lighthouses and field hospitals to those who might once have regarded them as peculiar and suspect. From the work and example of alternative forms of community, ultimately a different experience of political life might arise, grounded in the actual practice and mutual education of shared self-rule.

What we need today are practices fostered in local settings, focused on the creation of new and viable cultures, economics grounded in virtuosity within households, and the creation of civic polis life. Not a better theory, but better practices. Such a condition and differing philosophy that it encourage might finally be worthy of the name "liberal." After a five hundred–year philosophical experiment that has now run its course, the way is clear to building anew and better. The greatest proof of human freedom today lies in our ability to imagine, and build, liberty after liberalism.

Notes

PREFACE

1. Václav Havel, "The Power of the Powerless," in *Open Letters: Selected Writings, 1965–1990* (New York: Vintage, 1992), 162.

2. Wilson Carey McWilliams, "Democracy and the Citizen: Community, Dignity, and the Crisis of Contemporary Politics in America," in *Redeeming Democracy in America*, ed. Patrick J. Deneen and Susan J. McWilliams (Lawrence: University Press of Kansas, 2011), 27.

INTRODUCTION

1. Adrian Vermeule, *Law's Abnegation: From Law's Empire to the Administrative State* (Cambridge: Harvard University Press, 2016).

2. Thomas L. Friedman, *The Lexus and the Olive Tree* (New York: Anchor, 2000), 7.

3. From a response essay to David Brooks "Organization Kid," by a member of Notre Dame class of 2018, in my course Political Philosophy and Education, August 29, 2016. Paper in author's possession.

4. Wendell Berry, "Agriculture from the Roots Up," in *The Way of Ignorance and Other Essays* (Emeryville, CA: Shoemaker and Hoard, 2005), 107–8.

5. Nicholas Carr, *The Shallows: What the Internet Is Doing to Our Brains* (New York: Norton, 2010).

6. Sherry Turkle, *Alone Together: Why We Expect More from Technology and Less from Each Other* (New York: Basic, 2011).

7. Lee Silver, *Remaking Eden: How Genetic Engineering and Cloning Will Transform the Family* (New York: HarperPerennial, 1998); Mark Shiffman, "Humanity 4.5," *First Things*, November 2015.

CHAPTER 1. UNSUSTAINABLE LIBERALISM

An early version of parts of this chapter was previously published as "Unsustainable Liberalism" in *First Things*, August, 2012. I am grateful for permission to republish portions of that original essay.

1. The best guide to the premodern origins of many institutions commonly thought to have their origins in the early-modern liberal tradition remains Charles Howard McIlwain's *The Growth of Political Thought in the West: From the Greeks to the End of the Middle Ages* (New York: Macmillan, 1932). See also his *Constitutionalism, Ancient and Modern* (Ithaca, NY: Cornell University Press, 1940). Another helpful source is John Neville Figgis, *Studies of Political Thought: From Gerson to Grotius* (Cambridge: Cambridge University Press, 1907).

2. Brian Tierney, *The Idea of Natural Rights: Studies on Natural Rights, Natural Law, and Church Law, 1150–1625* (Grand Rapids, MI: Eerdmans, 1997); Paul E. Sigmund, *Natural Law in Political Thought* (Lanham, MD: University Press of America, 1981); Richard Tuck, *Natural Rights Theories: Their Origins and Development* (Cambridge: Cambridge University Press, 1982); Larry Siedentop, *Inventing the Individual: The Origins of Western Liberalism* (Cambridge: Harvard University Press, 2014).

3. Niccolò Machiavelli, *The Prince*, ed. and trans. David Wooton (Indianapolis: Hackett, 1995), 48.

4. Francis Bacon, *Of the Advancement of Learning*, in *The Works of Francis Bacon*, 14 vols., ed. James Spedding, Robert Leslie Ellis, and Douglas Denon Heath (London: Longmans, 1879), 3: 294–95.

5. Francis Fukuyama, "The End of History," *The National Interest*, Summer 1989.

6. Thomas Hobbes, *Leviathan*, ed. Edwin Curley (Indianapolis: Hackett, 1994), 229.

7. Ibid., 143.

8. John Locke, *Second Treatise of Government*, ed. C. B. MacPherson (Indianapolis: Hackett, 1980), 40.

9. Francis Bacon, *Valerius Terminus, Of the Interpretation of Nature*, in Spedding, Ellis, and Heath, *The Works of Francis Bacon*, 3: 218.

CHAPTER 2. UNITING
INDIVIDUALISM AND STATISM

1. Bill Bishop, *The Big Sort: Why the Clustering of Like-Minded America Is Tearing Us Apart* (New York: Houghton Mifflin Harcourt, 2008); Marc J. Dunkelman, *The Vanishing Neighbor: The Transformation of American Community* (New York: Norton, 2014); Charles A. Murray, *Coming Apart: The State of White America, 1960–2010* (New York: Crown Forum, 2012); Robert D. Putnam and David E. Campbell, *American Grace: How Religion Divides and Unites Us* (New York: Simon and Schuster, 2010).

2. Bertrand de Jouvenel, *The Pure Theory of Politics* (Indianapolis: Liberty Fund, 2000), 60.

3. Locke, *Second Treatise of Government*, ed. C. B. McPherson (Indianapolis: Hackett, 1980), 32.

4. Thus the Constitution positively charges Congress "to promote the Progress of sciences and useful arts."

5. John Stuart Mill, "Considerations on Representative Government," in *On Liberty and Other Essays*, ed. John Gray (Oxford: Oxford University Press, 2008), 232.

6. Karl Polanyi, *The Great Transformation: The Political Origins of Our Time* (Boston: Beacon, 2001). More recently, a similar argument has been made by Brad Gregory in his magisterial *The Unintended Reformation: How a Religious Revolution Secularized Society* (Cambridge: Belknap Press of Harvard University Press, 2012).

7. See especially Polanyi, *The Great Transformation*, 45–58.

8. Ibid., 147.

9. Among the most powerful indictments of industrialism are to be found in the writings of southern authors, and thereby often dismissed as defenses of an unjust economic order. See, for instance, The Twelve Southerners, *I'll Take My Stand: The South and the Agrarian Tradition* (New York: Harper, 1930), and Wendell Berry's response to this indictment in *The Hidden Wound* (Boston: Houghton Mifflin, 1970).

10. E. F. Schumacher, *Small Is Beautiful: Economics as if People Mattered* (New York: Harper and Row, 1975); Stephen Marglin, *The Dismal*

Science: How Thinking Like an Economist Undermines Community (Cambridge: Harvard University Press, 2008).

11. John M. Broder and Felicity Barringer, "The E.P.A. Says 17 States Can't Set Emission Rules, *New York Times*, December 20, 2007, http://www.nytimes.com/2007/12/20/washington/20epa.html?_r=0.

12. John Dewey, *Individualism, Old and New* (Prometheus, 1999), 37, 39.

13. Herbert Croly, *The Promise of American Life* (Cambridge: Harvard University Press, 1965), 280.

14. Walter Rauschenbusch, *Theology for the Social Gospel* (Louisville, KY: Westminster John Knox Press, 1997).

15. The Obama campaign's original "Life of Julia" ad has been removed from the campaign's website (https://www.barackobama.com/life-of-julia/). Most search results now direct one to various spoofs and critiques of the original ad. Stories about the ad are still available, and provide a general description of the campaign spot. See, for example, http://www.newyorker.com/news/daily-comment/oh-julia-from-birth-to-death-left-and-right.

16. Marglin, *The Dismal Science*.

17. Hannah Arendt, *Origins of Totalitarianism* (New York: Harcourt, Brace, 1951); Erich Fromm, *Escape from Freedom* (New York: Farrar and Rinehart, 1941); Robert A. Nisbet, *The Quest for Community: A Study in the Ethics of Order and Freedom* (Wilmington, DE: ISI, 2010). The publication record of *Quest for Community* is revealing. Published by Oxford University Press in 1953, it went out of print until the late 1960s, when it became popular with the New Left. Thereafter, it went out of print again until 2010, when it was republished—with a new introduction by conservative *New York Times* columnist Ross Douthat—by the conservative Intercollegiate Studies Institute press. Nisbet's argument has never found a true political home in America, wandering between the New Left and the social conservatives on the right. Yet that his book continues to find readers suggests that his analysis remains relevant, even with the eclipse and fall of fascism and communism. See E. J. Dionne, *Why Americans Hate Politics* (New York: Simon and Schuster, 1992), 36.

18. Nisbet, *The Quest for Community*, 145.

19. Alexis de Tocqueville, *Democracy in America*, trans. George Lawrence (New York: Harper and Row, 1969), 672.

CHAPTER 3. LIBERALISM AS ANTICULTURE

1. Mario Vargas Llosa, *Notes on the Death of Culture: Essays on Spectacle and Society* (New York: Farrar, Straus and Giroux, 2015), 58.

2. Polanyi, *The Great Transformation*. See also William T. Cavanaugh, "'Killing for the Telephone Company': Why the Nation-State Is Not the Keeper of the Common Good," in *Migrations of the Holy: God, State, and the Political Meaning of the Church* (Grand Rapids, MI: Eerdmans, 2011).

3. A quietly beautiful expression of this view, captured after its passing, is offered by the part-time political scientist and full-time Vermonter Charles Fish, who wrote of his farming forebears: "For Grandmother and my uncles, there was an imagined coexistence of the hand of God and the workings of nature that was midway between divinity and the operations of mechanical laws. They would have been uncomfortable if pressed to describe the relationship between the two or to declare whether they believed there was none. When weather or disease caused damage, it was nature, not God, that was named, but nature was not simply a malevolent force. While they had to fight her as she sought to dissolve the artful bonds which held things in useful forms, they also felt they were cooperating with her as they made use of her powers of renewal and growth. They would have listened without objection to the phrase 'harnessing the power of nature,' but it is unlikely that in their hearts they ever thought they could do it except in the most partial way. Through nature they could accomplish fine things, but that nature herself was ever under their control would have struck them as not quite blasphemous but erroneous and perhaps presumptuous. There was much to remind them that they were not the lords of creation. . . . What fell to their hands to do they did with all their strength and craft, but they knew they worked at the center of a mystery, the motions of which they could neither influence nor predict." Charles Fish, *In Good Hands: The Keeping of a Family Farm* (New York: Farrar, Straus and Giroux, 1995), 102–3.

4. John Dewey, *Reconstruction in Philosophy* (1920; New York: New American Library, 1950), 46.

5. Ibid., 48.

6. Tocqueville, *Democracy in America*, 508.

7. Ibid., 548.

8. Ibid., 557–58.

9. Thomas Hobbes, *On the Citizen*, ed. and trans. Richard Tuck and Michael Silverthorne (Cambridge: Cambridge University Press, 1998), 102.

10. Thomas Jefferson, *A Summary View of the Rights of British America. Set Forth in Some Resolutions Intended for the Inspection of the Present Delegates of the People of Virginia. Now in Convention. By a Native, and Member of the House of Burgesses.* (Williamsburg: Clementina Rind, 1774).

11. Berry's understanding is best grasped not through his essays but through his fiction. Based in the fictional location of Port William, Berry's fiction portrays an idyllic (though not perfect) communal setting in which strong ties between people and to place and land are its prominent features. As Berry has described his own fiction, "by means of the imagined place . . . I have learned to see my native landscape and neighborhood as a place unique in the world, a work of God, possessed of an inherent sanctity that mocks any human valuation that can be put on it." Berry, "Imagination in Place," in *The Way of Ignorance*, 50–51.

12. Wendell Berry, "Sex, Economy, Freedom, and Community," in *Sex, Economy, Freedom, and Community: Eight Essays* (New York: Pantheon, 1994), 120.

13. Ibid., 120–21.

14. Ibid., 157.

15. Lest it appear that this critique of liberal "standardization"—most often in the form of national, and increasingly international, legal imposition—implies that the left or Democratic Party is the sole perpetrator, see as a counterexample the article "Bullies along the Potomac" by Nina Mendelson in the *New York Times*, July 5, 2006, http://www.nytimes.com/2006/07/05/opinion/05mendelson.html. Mendelson relates that the Republican-controlled Congress—far from insisting upon states' rights—had in a five-year span beginning in 2001 enacted twenty-seven laws "that preempt state authority in areas from air pollution to consumer protection," including one law entitled the National Uniformity for Food Act. Or, in the domain of education, consider the standardizing effect of President Bush's landmark No Child Left Behind program, or attraction of the standardization in the area of higher education that was threatened by President Bush's secretary of education Margaret Spellings's Commission on the Future of Higher Education.

16. Berry's stance shares significant resemblance with many of the criticisms and concerns of the intellectual historian Christopher Lasch. See Lasch's *The True and Only Heaven: Progress and Its Critics* (New York: Norton, 1991) and *The Revolt of the Elites and the Betrayal of Democracy* (New York: Norton, 1994).

17. The defense of local diversity begins, but does not end, with agricultural diversity. Such diversity is necessary not only for reasons of good husbandry but further, as a means of avoiding the susceptibility of homogenous systems to cataclysmic events—whether natural or man-made, such as in the case of terrorism. See Berry, "Some Notes for the Kerry Campaign, If Wanted," *The Way of Ignorance*, 18. Berry was under little illusion that Kerry would heed his advice, and it seems he was correct in that estimation.

18. In this sense, Berry's critique of externally imposed "logic" is similar to the critiques of Michael Oakeshott. See "Rationalism in Politics," in *Rationalism in Politics and Other Essays* (New York: Basic, 1962), and *The Politics of Faith and the Politics of Scepticism* (New Haven: Yale University Press, 1996).

19. Aleksandr Solzhenitsyn, "A World Split Apart," in *Solzhenitsyn at Harvard*, ed. Ronald Berman (Washington, DC: Ethics and Public Policy Center, 1980), 7.

20. Stephen Gardner, "The Eros and Ambitions of Psychological Man," in Philip Rieff, *The Triumph of the Therapeutic: Uses of Faith after Freud* (Wilmington, DE: ISI, 2006), 244.

21. Simone Polillo, "Structuring Financial Elites: Conservative Banking and the Local Sources of Reputation in Italy and the United States, 1850–1914," Ph.D. diss., University of Pennsylvania, 2008, 157. This study was brought to my attention by Matthew Crawford in *Shop Class as Soul Craft: An Inquiry into the Value of Work* (New York: Penguin, 2010).

22. Cited in Polillo, "Structuring Financial Elites," 159.

23. "No Longer the Heart of the Home, the Piano Industry Quietly Declines," *New York Public Radio*, January 6, 2015, http://www.thetakeaway.org/story/despite-gradual-decline-piano-industry-stays-alive/.

CHAPTER 4. TECHNOLOGY AND THE LOSS OF LIBERTY

1. Brett T. Robinson, *Appletopia* (Waco, TX: Baylor University Press, 2013).

2. Nicholas Carr, *The Shallows: What the Internet Is Doing to our Brains* (New York: Norton, 2010).

3. Sherry Turkle, *Alone Together: Why We Expect More from Technology and Less from Each Other* (New York: Basic, 2011).

4. Neil Postman, *Technopoly: The Surrender of Culture to Technology* (New York: Vintage, 1993).

5. Ibid., 28.

6. Francis Fukuyama, *The End of History and the Last Man* (New York: Free Press, 1992); Francis Fukuyama, *Our Posthuman Future: Consequences of the Biotechnology Revolution* (New York: Farrar, Straus and Giroux, 2002).

7. Daniel J. Boorstin, *The Republic of Technology: Reflections on Our Future Community* (New York: Harper and Row, 1978), 5.

8. Stephen Marche, "Is Facebook Making Us Lonely?" *Atlantic*, May, 2012.

9. Richard H. Thomas, "From Porch to Patio," *Palimpsest*, August 1975.

10. This practice echoes the call by John Winthrop in his oft-cited but rarely read sermon "A Model of Christian Charity" for the kind of community by the emigrating Puritans whose members would be knit closely together in the bonds of Christian charity: "Now the only way to avoid this shipwreck, and to provide for our posterity, is to follow the counsel of Micah, to do justly, to love mercy, to walk humbly with our God. For this end, we must be knit together, in this work, as one man. We must entertain each other in brotherly affection. We must be willing to abridge ourselves of our superfluities, for the supply of others' necessities. We must uphold a familiar commerce together in all meekness, gentleness, patience and liberality. We must delight in each other; make others' conditions our own; rejoice together, mourn together, labor and suffer together, always having before our eyes our commission and community in the work, as members of the same body." John Winthrop, "A Model of Christian Charity," in *The American Puritans: Their Prose and Poetry*, ed. Perry Miller (New York: Columbia University Press, 1982), 83.

11. Stephen Marglin, *The Dismal Science: How Thinking Like an Economist Undermines Community* (Cambridge: Harvard University Press, 2008), 18.

12. Boorstin, *The Republic of Technology*, 9.

CHAPTER 5. LIBERALISM AGAINST LIBERAL ARTS

1. Clark Kerr, *The Uses of the University*, 5th ed. (Cambridge: Harvard University Press, 2001), 199.

2. https://www.utexas.edu/about/mission-and-values.

3. In his classic statement about *The Two Cultures*, C. P. Snow is able to justify with ease why humanists should study the sciences but struggles to articulate grounds why scientists should study the humanities. C. P. Snow, *The Two Cultures* (Cambridge: Cambridge University Press, 1965).

4. See the contrast drawn by Ruthellen Josselson between "the hermeneutics of faith and the hermeneutics of suspicion," in "The Hermeneutics of Faith and the Hermeneutics of Suspicion," *Narrative Inquiry* 14, no. 1 (2004): 1–28.

5. For a fuller discussion of this history, see Anthony Kronman, *Education's End: Why Our Colleges and Universities Have Given Up on the Meaning of Life* (New Haven: Yale University Press, 2006), especially chapters 3–4.

6. A *locus classicus* that wed radical feminism with optimistic belief in technology's ability to alter human nature remains Shulamith Firestone, *The Dialectic of Sex* (New York: Morrow, 1970).

7. Steven Levy, "GU NAACP President Discusses Diversity Issues," *Hoya*, October 19, 2010. "I feel [that] money and the lack of it, as well as the lack of opportunity to participate in our consumerist, capitalist society and economy, proves difficult. For many minorities, they find that they're not located on the same playing field as the rest of the nation." http://www.thehoya.com/gu-naacp-president-discusses-diversity-issues/#.

One study has shown that there is a significant disadvantage in elite college admissions for students who have held leadership positions in areas that do not conform to expectations of "capitalist society." Russell Nieli summarizes the study: "Participation in such Red State activities as high school ROTC, 4-H clubs, or the Future Farmers of America was found to reduce very substantially a student's chances of gaining admission to the competitive private colleges in the NSCE database on an all-other-things-considered basis. The admissions disadvantage was greatest for those in leadership positions in these activities or those winning honors and awards. Being an officer or winning awards 'for such career-oriented activities as junior ROTC, 4-H, or Future Farmers of America,' say Espenshade and Radford, 'has a significantly negative association with admission outcomes at highly selective institutions.' Excelling in these activities 'is associated with 60 or 65 percent lower odds of admission.' " Russell Nieli, "How Diversity Punishes Asians, Poor Whites, and Lots of Others," Minding the Campus, July 12, 2010. https://www.princeton.edu/~tje/files/Pub_Minding%20the%20campus%20combined%20files.pdf.

8. Wilson Carey McWilliams, "Politics," *American Quarterly* 35, nos. 1–2 (1983): 27. A recent confirmation of this assessment can be found in this statement by political scientist James Stimson: "When we observe the behavior of those who live in distressed areas, we are observing not the effect of decline on the working class, we are observing a highly selected group of people who faced economic adversity and chose to stay at home and accept it when others sought and found opportunity elsewhere. . . . Those who are fearful, conservative, in the social sense, and lack ambition stay and accept decline." In other words, the disadvantaged status of the white working class is the workers' own fault. Cited by Thomas B. Edsall, "The Closing of the Republican Mind," *New York Times*, July 13, 2017. https://www.nytimes.com/2017/07/13/opinion/republicans-elites-trump.html.

9. Matt Reed, a community college dean, acknowledged his opposition to the likes of Allan Bloom in the 1980s, but wonders where such conservative defenders of the humanities have gone in the wake of aggressive financial cutbacks in the humanities by conservative legislators: "I can only imagine Allan Bloom's response to the Florida bill. Any conservative culture warrior worthy of the name should be apoplectic at the idea of letting legislators dictate curriculum. At this point, conservatives have given up on the idea of maintaining an intellectual tradition, and have settled on cost reduction as a good in itself. They've decided that rather than defending Edmund Burke, it's easier just to run Intro to Business online and call it a day." "Remember the Canon Wars?" Inside Higher Ed, April 11, 2013, https://www.insidehighered.com/blogs/confessions-community-college-dean/remember-canon-wars. See also Jonathan Marks, "Conservatives and the Higher Ed 'Bubble,' " Inside Higher Ed, November 15, 2012, https://www.insidehighered.com/views/2012/11/15/conservative-focus-higher-ed-bubble-undermines-liberal-education-essay.

10. The history of institutional name changes is instructive: https://en.wikipedia.org/wiki/List_of_university_and_college_name_changes_in_the_United_States.

11. Wendell Berry, "Faustian Economics: Hell Hath No Limits," *Harper's*, May 2008, 37–38.

CHAPTER 6. THE NEW ARISTOCRACY

1. Murray, *Coming Apart*.

2. Locke, *Second Treatise of Government*, 23, 26.

3. F. A. Hayek, *The Constitution of Liberty*, ed. Ronald Hamowy (Chicago: University of Chicago Press, 2011), 96.

4. Ibid., 95–96.

5. Tyler Cowen, *Average Is Over: Powering America Past the Age of the Great Stagnation* (New York: Dutton, 2013), 258.

6. Ibid.

7. John Stuart Mill, *On Liberty*, in Gray, *On Liberty and Other Essays*, 12–13.

8. Ibid., 65.

9. Ibid., 67.

10. Ibid., 68.

11. Ibid., 72.

12. Edmund Burke, *Reflections on the Revolution in France*, ed. J. G. A. Pocock (Indianapolis: Hackett, 1987), 76.

13. Ibid., 29, 49.

14. Robert B. Reich, "Secession of the Successful," *New York Times*, January 20, 1991; Christopher Lasch, *The Revolt of the Elite and the Betrayal of Democracy* (New York: Norton, 1994).

15. Murray, *Coming Apart;* Robert A. Putnam, *Our Kids: The American Dream in Crisis* (New York: Simon and Schuster, 2015).

CHAPTER 7. THE DEGRADATION OF CITIZENSHIP

1. Fareed Zakaria, "The Rise of Illiberal Democracy," *Foreign Affairs*, November–December, 1997, 22–43. Zakaria subsequently expanded this essay in his book *The Future of Freedom: Illiberal Democracy at Home and Abroad* (New York: Norton, 2007).

2. William Galston, "The Growing Threat of Illiberal Democracy," *Wall Street Journal*, January 3, 2017, http://www.wsj.com/articles/the-growing-threat-of-illiberal-democracy-1483488245.

3. Jason Brennan, *Against Democracy* (Princeton: Princeton University Press, 2016). In the wake of the 2016 election of Donald Trump, Brennan wrote in a *Washington Post* article, "Most voters are systematically misinformed about the basic facts relevant to elections, and many advocate policies they would reject if they were better informed. We get low-quality government because voters have little idea what they are doing"; "The Problem with Our Government Is Democracy."

4. Bryan Caplan, *The Myth of the Rational Voter: Why Democracies Choose Bad Policies* (Princeton: Princeton University Press, 2007); Jeffrey Friedman, "Democratic Incompetence in Normative and Positive Theory: Neglected Implications of 'The Nature of Belief Systems in Mass Publics,'" *Critical Review* 18, nos. 1–3 (2006): i–xliii; Damon Root, *Overruled: The Long War over Control of the U.S. Supreme Court* (New York: St. Martin's, 2014).

5. Edward A. Purcell, *The Crisis of Democratic Theory: Scientific Naturalism and the Problem of Value* (Lexington: University Press of Kentucky, 1973), 98.

6. Walter J. Shepard, "Democracy in Transition," *American Political Science Review* 29 (1935): 9.

7. Ibid., 18.

8. John Dewey, *The Public and Its Problems* (1927; Athens, Ohio: Swallow, 1954), 183–84.

9. John Dewey, "My Pedagogic Creed," in *The Early Works of John Dewey, 1882–1898*, ed. Jo Ann Boydston, vol. 5 (Carbondale: Southern Illinois University Press, 1967–72).

10. Quoted in Purcell, *The Crisis of Democratic Theory*, 95.

11. Quoted ibid., 103.

12. James Madison, Alexander Hamilton, and John Jay, *The Federalist*, ed. George W. Carey and James McClellan (Indianapolis: Liberty Fund, 2001), no. 10, p. 46.

13. Ibid.; emphasis mine.

14. Ibid., no. 34, p. 163.

15. Ibid., no. 34, p. 164.

16. Ibid., no. 17, p. 80.

17. Ibid., no. 46, p. 243; ibid., no. 17, p. 81.

18. Ibid., no. 17, p. 81; emphasis mine.

19. Ibid., no. 46, p. 244.

20. Ibid., no. 27, p. 133; emphasis mine.

21. "It is no accident that the growing organization of democracy coincides with the rise of science, including the machinery of the telegraph and locomotive for distributing truth. There is but one fact—the more complete movement of man to his unity with his fellows through realizing the truth of life"; John Dewey, "Christianity and Democracy," in Boydston, *Early Works*, 4: 9.

22. Tocqueville, *Democracy in America*, 243.

23. Ibid.

24. Quoted ibid., 46.

25. Ibid., 515.

26. Ibid., 57.

27. Ibid., 243–44.

28. Jason Brennan writes, "[The] decline in political engagement is a *good start*, but we still have a long way to go. We should hope for even less participation, not more. Ideally, politics would occupy only a small portion of the average person's attention. Ideally, most people would fill their days with painting, poetry, music, architecture, statuary, tapestry, and porcelain, or perhaps football, NASCAR, tractor pulls, celebrity gossip, and trips to Applebee's. Most people, ideally, would not worry about politics at all." Brennan, *Against Democracy*, 3.

CONCLUSION

1. Wendell Berry, "Feminism, the Body and the Machine," in *What Are People For?* (New York: North Point, 1990); Nancy Fraser, *Fortunes of Feminism: From State-Managed Capitalism to Neo-Liberal Crisis* (New York: Verso, 2013).

2. Cavanaugh, " 'Killing for the Telephone Company.' "

3. In addition to aggressive efforts to narrowly define religious freedom as "freedom of worship" under the Obama administration, consider efforts to define the relationship of parents and children in liberal political terms and thus to put them under the supervision of the state. See, for instance, Samantha Goldwin, "Against Parental Rights," *Columbia Law Review* 47, no. 1 (2015).

4. Tom Shachtman, *Rumspringa: To Be or Not to Be Amish* (New York: North Point, 2007).

5. Rod Dreher, *The Benedict Option: A Strategy for Christians in a Post-Christian Nation* (New York: Sentinel, 2017).

6. Shannon Hayes, *Radical Homemakers: Reclaiming Domesticity from a Consumer Culture* (Left to Right, 2010).

7. Tocqueville, *Democracy in America*, 510.

Bibliography

Arendt, Hannah. *The Origins of Totalitarianism.* New York: Harcourt, Brace, 1951.

Bacon, Francis. *Of the Advancement of Learning.* In *The Works of Francis Bacon*, 14 vol, ed. James Spedding, Robert Leslie Ellis and Douglas Denon Heath. London: Longmans, 1879.

——. *Valerius Terminus, "Of the Interpretation of Nature."* In Spedding, Ellis and Heath, *The Works of Francis Bacon.*

Barringer, Felicity, and John M. Broder. "E.P.A. Says 17 States Can't Set Emission Rules." *New York Times*, December 20, 2007.

Berry, Wendell. "Agriculture from the Roots Up." In *The Way of Ignorance: And Other Essays.* Emeryville, CA: Shoemaker and Hoard, 2005.

——. "Faustian Economics: Hell Hath No Limits." *Harper's*, May 2008, 37–38.

——. "Feminism, the Body and the Machine." In *What Are People For?* Berkeley, CA: Counterpoint, 1990.

——. *The Hidden Wound.* Boston: Houghton Mifflin, 1970.

——. *Sex, Economy, Freedom, and Community: Eight Essays.* New York: Pantheon, 1994.

Bishop, Bill. *The Big Sort: Why the Clustering of Like-Minded America Is Tearing Us Apart.* New York: Houghton Mifflin Harcourt, 2008.

Bloom, Allan. *The Closing of the American Mind: How Higher Education Has Failed Democracy and Impoverished the Souls of Today's Students.* New York: Simon and Schuster, 1987.

Boorstin, Daniel J. *The Republic of Technology: Reflections on Our Future Community.* New York: Harper and Row, 1978.

Brennan, Jason. *Against Democracy.* Princeton: Princeton University Press, 2016.

——. "The Problem with Our Government Is Democracy." *Washington Post*, November 10, 2016.

Burke, Edmund. *Reflections on the Revolution in France*, ed. J. G. A. Pocock. 1790; Indianapolis: Hackett, 1987.

Caplan, Bryan. *The Myth of the Rational Voter: Why Democracies Choose Bad Policies.* Princeton: Princeton University Press, 2007.

Carr, Nicholas G. *The Shallows: What the Internet Is Doing to our Brains.* New York: Norton, 2010.

Cavanaugh, William T. "'Killing for the Telephone Company': Why the Nation-State Is Not the Keeper of the Common Good." In *Migrations of the Holy: God, State, and the Political Meaning of the Church.* Grand Rapids, MI: Eerdmans, 2011.

Cowen, Tyler. *Average Is Over: Powering America Past the Age of the Great Stagnation.* New York: Dutton, 2013.

Crawford, Matthew. *Shop Class as Soul Craft: An Inquiry into the Value of Work.* New York: Penguin, 2010.

Croly, Herbert. *The Promise of American Life.* 1909; Cambridge: Harvard University Press, 1965.

Deneen, Patrick. "Against Great Books: Questioning our Approach to the Western Canon." *First Things*, January 2013.

Dewey, John. *The Early Works of John Dewey, 1882–1898.* Vol. 5, ed. Jo Ann Boydston. Carbondale: Southern Illinois University Press, 1967–72.

——. *Individualism, Old and New.* 1930; Amherst, NY: Prometheus, 1999.

——. *The Public and Its Problems.* 1927; Athens, Ohio: Swallow, 1954.

——. *Reconstruction in Philosophy.* London: University of London Press, 1921.

Dionne, E. J., Jr. *Why Americans Hate Politics.* New York: Simon and Schuster, 1992.

Dreher, Rod. *The Benedict Option: A Strategy for Christians in a Post-Christian Nation.* New York: Sentinel, 2017.

Dunkelman, Marc J. *The Vanishing Neighbor: The Transformation of American Community.* New York: Norton, 2014.

Figgis, John Neville. *Studies of Political Thought: From Gerson to Grotius.* Cambridge: Cambridge University Press, 1907.

Firestone, Shulamith. *The Dialectic of Sex: The Case for Feminist Revolution.* New York: Bantam, 1971.

Fish, Charles. *In Good Hands: The Keeping of a Family Farm.* New York: Farrar, Straus and Giroux, 1995.

Foucault, Michel. *The Order of Things: An Archaeology of the Human Sciences.* New York: Vintage, 1994.

Fraser, Nancy. *Fortunes of Feminism: From State-Managed Capitalism to Neo-Liberal Crisis.* New York: Verso, 2013.

Friedman, Jeffrey. "Democratic Incompetence in Normative and Positive Theory: Neglected Implications of 'The Nature of Belief Systems in Mass Publics.'" *Critical Review* 18, nos. 1–3 (2006): i–xliii.

Friedman, Thomas L. *The Lexus and the Olive Tree.* New York: Farrar, Straus and Giroux, 1999.

Fromm, Erich. *Escape from Freedom.* New York: Farrar and Rinehart, 1941.

Fukuyama, Francis. "The End of History?" *National Interest,* Summer 1989.

———. *The End of History and the Last Man.* New York: Free Press, 1992.

———. *Our Posthuman Future: Consequences of the Biotechnology Revolution.* New York: Farrar, Straus and Giroux, 2002.

Galston, William. "The Growing Threat of Illiberal Democracy." *Wall Street Journal,* January 3, 2017.

Gardner, Stephen. "The Eros and Ambitions of Psychological Man." In Philip Rieff, *The Triumph of the Therapeutic: Uses of Faith after Freud,* 40th anniversary ed. Wilmington, DE: ISI, 2006.

Goldwin, Samantha. "Against Parental Rights." *Columbia Law Review* 47, no. 1 (2015).

Gregory, Brad S. *The Unintended Reformation: How a Religious Revolution Secularized Society.* Cambridge: Belknap Press of Harvard University Press, 2012.

Habermas, Jürgen. *Legitimation Crisis*, trans. Thomas McCarthy. Boston: Beacon, 1975.

Hanson, Victor Davis, and John Heath. *Who Killed Homer: The Demise of Classical Education and the Recovery of Greek Wisdom.* New York: Free Press, 1998.

Havel, Vaclav. "The Power of the Powerless." In *Open Letters: Selected Writings, 1965–1990.* New York: Vintage, 1992.

Hayek, F. A. *The Constitution of Liberty*, ed. Ronald Hamowy. Chicago: University of Chicago Press, 2011.

Hayes, Shannon. *Radical Homemakers: Reclaiming Domesticity from a Consumer Culture.* Left to Right, 2010.

Hobbes, Thomas. *Leviathan*, ed. Edwin Curley. 1651; Indianapolis: Hackett, 1994.

———. *On the Citizen*, ed. and trans. Richard Tuck and Michael Silverthorne. 1642 Cambridge: Cambridge University Press, 1998.

Jefferson, Thomas. *A Summary View of the Rights of British America. Set Forth in Some Resolutions Intended for the Inspection of the Present Delegates of the People of Virginia. Now in Convention. By a Native, and Member of the House of Burgesses.* Williamsburg: Clementina Rind, 1774.

Josselson, Ruthellen. "The Hermeneutics of Faith and the Hermeneutics of Suspicion." *Narrative Inquiry* 14, no. 1 (2004): 1–28.

Jouvenel, Bertrand de. *The Pure Theory of Politics.* Indianapolis: Liberty Fund, 2000.

Kerr, Clark. *The Uses of the University*, 5th ed. Cambridge: Harvard University Press, 2001.

Korn, Sandra Y. L. "The Doctrine of Academic Freedom." *Harvard Crimson*, February 18, 2014.

Kronman, Anthony. *Education's End: Why Our Colleges and Universities Have Given Up on the Meaning of Life.* New Haven: Yale University Press, 2006.

Lasch, Christopher. *The Revolt of the Elites and the Betrayal of Democracy.* New York: Norton, 1994.

———. *The True and Only Heaven: Progress and Its Critics.* New York: Norton, 1991.

Lepore, Jill. "Oh, Julia: From Birth to Death, Left and Right." *New Yorker*, May 7, 2012.

Levin, Yuval. *The Great Debate: Edmund Burke, Thomas Paine, and the Birth of Right and Left.* New York: Basic, 2014.

Levy, Stephen. "GU NAACP President Discusses Diversity Issues." *Hoya,* October 19, 2010.

Lipset, Seymour M. *Political Man: The Social Bases of Politics.* Garden City, NY: Doubleday, 1960.

Locke, John. *Second Treatise of Government,* ed. C. B. MacPherson. 1689; Indianapolis: Hackett, 1980.

Lukianoff, Greg, and Jonathan Haidt. "The Coddling of the American Mind." *Atlantic,* July 2015.

Machiavelli, Niccolò. *The Prince,* ed. and trans. David Wooton. Indianapolis: Hackett, 1995.

Marche, Stephen. "Is Facebook Making Us Lonely?" *Atlantic,* May 2012.

Marglin, Stephen. *The Dismal Science: How Thinking Like an Economist Undermines Community.* Cambridge: Harvard University Press, 2008.

Marks, Jonathan. "Conservatives and the Higher Ed 'Bubble.'" Inside Higher Ed, November 15, 2012.

McIlwain, Charles Howard. *Constitutionalism, Ancient and Modern.* Ithaca, NY: Cornell University Press, 1940.

——. *The Growth of Political Thought in the West: From the Greeks to the End of the Middle Ages.* New York: Macmillan, 1932.

McWilliams, Wilson Carey. "Democracy and the Citizen: Community, Dignity, and the Crisis of Contemporary Politics in America." In *Redeeming Democracy in America,* ed. Patrick J. Deneen and Susan J. McWilliams. Lawrence: University Press of Kansas, 2011.

——. "Politics." *American Quarterly* 35, nos. 1–2 (1983): 19–38.

Mendelson, Nina. "Bullies along the Potomac." *New York Times,* July 5, 2006.

Mill, John Stuart. "Considerations on Representative Government." In *On Liberty and Other Essays,* ed. John Gray. Oxford: Oxford University Press, 2008.

Murray, Charles A. *Coming Apart: The State of White America, 1960–2010.* New York: Crown Forum, 2012.

Nieli, Russell K. "How Diversity Punishes Asians, Poor Whites, and Lots of Others." Minding the Campus, July 12, 2010.

Nisbet, Robert A. *The Quest for Community: A Study in the Ethics of Order and Freedom.* Wilmington, DE: ISI, 2010.

"No Longer the Heart of the Home, the Piano Industry Quietly Declines." *New York Public Radio,* January 6, 2015.

Oakeshott, Michael. *The Politics of Faith and the Politics of Scepticism.* New Haven: Yale University Press, 1996.

———. *Rationalism in Politics and Other Essays.* New York: Basic, 1962.

Polanyi, Karl. *The Great Transformation: The Political Origins of Our Time.* 1944; Boston: Beacon, 2001.

Polillo, Simone. "Structuring Financial Elites: Conservative Banking and the Local Sources of Reputation in Italy and the United States, 1850–1914." Ph.D. diss., University of Pennsylvania, 2008.

Postman, Neil. *Technopoly: The Surrender of Culture to Technology.* New York: Vintage, 1993.

Purcell, Edward A. *The Crisis of Democratic Theory: Scientific Naturalism and the Problem of Value.* Lexington: University Press of Kentucky, 1973.

Putnam, Robert D. *Our Kids: The American Dream in Crisis.* New York: Simon and Schuster, 2015.

Putnam, Robert D., and David E. Campbell. *American Grace: How Religion Divides and Unites Us.* New York: Simon and Schuster, 2010.

Rauschenbusch, Walter. *Theology for the Social Gospel.* 1917; Louisville, KY: Westminster John Knox Press, 1997.

Reed, Matt. "Remember the Canon Wars?" Inside Higher Ed, April 11, 2013.

Reich, Robert B. "Secession of the Successful." *New York Times,* January 20, 1991.

Robinson, Brett T. *Appletopia: Media Technology and the Religious Imagination of Steve Jobs.* Waco, TX: Baylor University Press, 2013.

Root, Damon. *Overruled: The Long War for Control of the U.S. Supreme Court.* New York: St. Martin's, 2014.

Schumacher, E. F. *Small Is Beautiful: Economics as if People Mattered.* New York: Harper and Row, 1975.

Shachtman, Tom. *Rumspringa: To Be or Not to Be Amish.* New York: North Point, 2007.

Shepard, Walter J. "Democracy in Transition." *American Political Science Review* 29 (1935).

Shiffman, Mark. "Humanity 4.5," *First Things*, November, 2015.

Siedentop, Larry. *Inventing the Individual: The Origins of Western Liberalism*. Cambridge: Harvard University Press, 2014.

Sigmund, Paul E. *Natural Law in Political Thought*. Lanham, MD: University Press of America, 1981.

Silver, Lee M. *Remaking Eden: Cloning and beyond in a Brave New World*. New York: Avon, 1997.

Snow, C. P. *The Two Cultures*. Cambridge: Cambridge University Press, 1965.

Solzhenitsyn, Aleksandr. "The World Split Apart." In *Solzhenitsyn at Harvard*, ed. Ronald Berman. Washington, DC: Ethics and Public Policy Center, 1980.

Thomas, Richard H. "From Porch to Patio." *Palimpsest*, August 1975.

Tierney, Brian. *The Idea of Natural Rights: Studies on Natural Rights, Natural Law, and Church Law, 1150–1625*. Grand Rapids, MI: Eerdmans, 1997.

Tocqueville, Alexis de. *Democracy in America*, trans. George Lawrence. New York: Harper and Row, 1969.

Tuck, Richard. *Natural Rights Theories: Their Origins and Development*. Cambridge: Cambridge University Press, 1982.

Turkle, Sherry. *Alone Together: Why We Expect More from Technology and Less from Each Other*. New York: Basic, 2011.

Twelve Southerners. *I'll Take My Stand: The South and the Agrarian Tradition*. New York: Harper, 1930.

Vargas Llosa, Mario. *Notes on the Death of Culture: Essays on Spectacle and Society*. New York: Farrar, Straus and Giroux, 2015.

Vermeule, Adrian. *Law's Abnegation: From Law's Empire to the Administrative State*. Cambridge: Harvard University Press, 2016.

Winthrop, John. "A Model of Christian Charity." In *The American Puritans: Their Prose and Poetry*, ed. Perry Miller. New York: Columbia University Press, 1982.

Zakaria, Fareed. *The Future of Freedom: Illiberal Democracy at Home and Abroad*. New York: Norton, 2007.

——. "The Rise of Illiberal Democracy." *Foreign Affairs*, November–December, 1997.

Index

INDEX

computers, 15
consent, 188–90
conservatives: Constitution invoked
by, 18, 169; environmental
standards attacked by, 53; liberal
goals advanced by, 19, 35–37, 46,
83, 120; markets revered by, 45, 53,
58, 63; mastery of nature sought
by, 36–37, 72; sexual revolution vs.,
171; statism decried by, 45, 58;
traditional curriculum and, 120,
124–25
*Considerations on Representative
Government* (Mill), 50
Constitution, U.S., 18, 101, 162, 167,
169, 170
constitutionalism, 23, 31
consumerism, 65, 194
Copts, 122
courts, 1
Cowen, Tyler, 140–41
Crawford, Matthew, 88–89
Crisis of Democratic Theory, The
(Purcell), 158
"critical thinking," 115, 130
Croly, Herbert, 54–56

Dante Alighieri, 112
"deep state," 181
Democracy in America (Tocqueville),
61–62, 174, 181
democratic competence, 159, 161–62
depersonalization, 16–17
Descartes, René, 25–26, 81
Dewey, A. Gordon, 160
Dewey, John: custom and tradition
devalued by, 71–72; democracy
viewed by, 159, 173; human
perfectibility viewed by, 36, 54, 55;
as individualist, 47, 54, 56; as
statist, 45, 47, 55
Dismal Science, The (Marglin), 107
diversity, 18, 89, 111, 122, 124, 132
"diversity of faculties," 142, 166, 168,
171
"Do Machines Make History?"
(Heilbroner), 98
Douthat, Ross, 202n17
Dreher, Rod, 191

education, 110–30
elections, 1, 3, 168, 176; diminished
faith in, 2; Locke's proposals for,
146–47; presidential, 8; proposals
to restrict, 158–59; turnout in,
195
Ellul, Jacques, 95
"End of History, The" (Fukuyama),
28, 97
environmentalism, 14, 53, 109, 111
epistocracy, 157
Escape from Freedom (Fromm), 59
Ethics (Aristotle), 35
European Union, 156
executive branch, 8, 144–45

Facebook, 103–4
factions, 102, 163, 165
fascism, 5, 60, 181
federalism, 23, 169
Federalist, 101, 142, 162, 163, 167, 169,
171
Federal Reserve, 166
financial crisis, 85–88, 109, 126–27,
132
Firestone, Shulamith, 207n6
Fish, Charles, 203n3
Frankenstein (Shelley), 92
Fraser, Nancy, 187
freedom of association, 7
free speech, 3, 7, 124
French Revolution, 43
Friedman, Jeffrey, 157, 158
Friedman, Thomas, 10
Fromm, Erich, 59
"From Porch to Patio" (Thomas),
105
Fukuyama, Francis, 21, 28, 97–98

Galston, William, 156
Gardner, Stephen, 84
Germany, 181
globalization, 12–13, 28, 30, 65, 132;
alienation heightened by, 3, 10,
178; conservative support for, 63;
criticism of, 53; inexorability of, 10,
14, 98
Goldwater, Barry, 172
"Great Books," 120, 125